BISHOP BRENDAN COMISKEY

G000099384

IT COULD
HAPPEN TO
A BISHOP

CAMPUS PUBLISHING

ISBN 1 873223 10 2

First Published March 1991

The author and publishers are grateful to *The Irish Catholic* for permission to reprint these pieces.

Print origination by Irish Typesetters, Galway

Printed in Ireland by Colour Books Ltd.

Published by
Campus Publishing Limited
26 Tirellan Heights
Galway
Ireland

Contents

Introduction

When the publisher of this book selected these various bits and pieces from my articles written over the past ten years, mostly in the *Irish Catholic*, he asked me to review them and to write this Introduction. I had forgotten many of the events about which I wrote and most of the little stories, parables, etc. which I had picked up along the way.

Some of them brought back bitter-sweet memories of men and women who peopled my life and who have gone to their eternal reward. I'm glad to have these written memories of them. Many of the other pieces are about seasons and times in my own life and in the life of the Church which I love.

Writing a weekly article for a paper is "brutal" when it is something that has to be squeezed into an already fairly busy schedule. Many of these were written far from home, on planes and trains, in airport lounges and hotel rooms, in Asia and America. Practically all of them were written "on the run", and most probably show every sign of it!

Some people would love to write if they had the time, or they will write a book "some day" . . . when they retire, perhaps. They won't, of course, and neither will anybody else who isn't writing a little bit "along the way". It's a great pity that more people don't write a little, a few lines in a diary, perhaps—not so much to set down what one did that day, but how one reacted to the day's particular events. Events may be important but people's reactions to and feelings about events are much more fascinating.

I remain convinced that there is no substitute for story. Tell a story and every listener will paint a picture and locate himself or herself within its frame. The very fact that there are so many stories in this book is proof enough that stories are remembered long after commentary on them has been forgotten. Story is as fascinating for the three-year-old as for the thirty-year-old, for the nine-year-old as for the ninety-year old.

In a so-called "information age", where gathering round the fire has been replaced by gathering round the "entertainment centre' in the home, a good story will still break through "canned amuse-ment". Story-telling is as simple as it is profound. Life itself is story-making: each one of us writes his or her story on every day's new page. Every single person's story is worth telling and is worth listening to.

I hope you enjoy some of the stories in this book. There is, I hope, more story and less "preaching" in the bad sense of the latter term. Many other people's stories are recounted in this book. I don't apologise for using these, for we are all of us part of each other's story and Jesus himself is the best story of all. He remains our "Good News", Gospel.

✝ Brendan Comiskey

It Could (Did!) Happen to A Bishop

As soon as some people hear that you are a bishop, they cannot wait to tell you "the one about the bishop." I can't see why I shouldn't get my own back and tell you a few stories I've heard about bishops. They actually happened (I think!).

Run or Resign

One of the hardest tasks a bishop has to do is to ask for and accept the resignation of a priest from his office as parish priest. The reasons are old age and the increasing demands made on such a man in today's rapidly changing Church and world.

It's not that such a man is being asked to retire from the priesthood or even priestly ministry. Just from one particular form of that ministry which makes too heavy demands on an aging constitution.

My first story is of a Scottish prelate who visited an old and revered priest-friend and with the greatest sense of delicacy and affection inquired whether the time had not come to consider resigning as parish priest.

It was a beautiful summer's afternoon and the old priest gazed out on the garden of the presbytery where he had spent so many busy and happy hours.

"Will you come out into the garden for a walk?" he asked his bishop.

Once outside, the parish priest pointed down to the bottom of the garden.

"Do you see that oak tree, Your Grace?" asked the parish priest. "Well, here's my answer to your question. The last man to run to that tree and back will resign!"

My story-teller informed me that both were still in office at the time of our talking!

The Real Thing

Closer to home there are two stories going the rounds, both of them about two of my brother bishops from the Armagh Province.

It would appear that one of them was standing on the steps of a church after finishing a Confirmation ceremony.

As he chatted with the newly confirmed and their parents, he felt a few quite distinctive tugs on his crozier. Looking down he soon confirmed that his crozier was being minutely examined by a youth of not more than ten years.

As it turned out the boy had had a brother or sister confirmed that day and the bishop discovered they belonged to a family well-known for dealing in metal and scrap iron.

This hardly prepared the prelate for the question from the youngster still examining the crozier. "Please, Father, is that real copper?"

Most Reverend

And the third story—also true—concerns a certain bishop being delayed on the border at an English Army checkpoint. By ordinary standards the young soldier seemed to be overdoing the delaying tactics, taking an extraordinary amount of time to examine the bishop's driving licence.

"Tell me, Padre," asked the soldier nonchalantly, "what does this "Most Reverend" mean on your licence? I get a lot of "Reverends" crossing here, but I'm curious to know what a "Most Reverend" means."

"To you," replied the bishop with barely concealed exasperation, "it means Colonel!"

Do We Still Believe?

The story is told of a man who was known to be very religious, great for saying prayers, and attending church regularly. He was not reluctant to remind people to put all their faith in God no matter what the circumstances.

The winter floods came to the village in which this man lived and no one could remember anything like it before. The water flowed into the houses to the extent that the local authorities decided to evacuate the village completely. But our friend decided to put his trust in God and remain behind.

"God will not abandon me," he said.

The water levels rose and rescue came in the form of a huge truck, ploughing its way through the rising waters, but the man stood his ground.

"God will not abandon me," he told his would-be rescuers. He alone remained behind.

As the waters continued to rise towards the second floor, the police came by in a boat, pleading with him to leave, but he simply repeated: "God will not abandon me!"

But the waters rose and rose, forcing him finally to climb out onto the roof of the house. An army helicopter made one last brave attempt but the man remained steadfast: "God will not abandon me!"

Still, the waters continued to rise and the man drowned. Next we see him before the judgement seat of God. Having received a merciful judgement, he couldn't help lodging a complaint with the Almighty: he felt a little disappointed with the divine response to his prayers for help down below.

"I always believed that faith could move mountains, but in my moment of greatest need, You did nothing for me," he said to God.

But God replied, "What do you mean 'I did nothing for you?' Didn't I send you a lorry, a boat and a helicopter? What more could I have done for you?"

The problem with that poor man's faith was that he couldn't see in real life what was happening; he couldn't make connections between his faith and the real world in which he lived. God and God's work were clear enough to him in times of prayer, when he was in church, but, for him, God was not in the bits and pieces of every day.

Cardinal O'Fiaich, in an address some years ago, to a Synod in Rome, borrowed from a little South Armagh children's rhyme to describe the same failure to make faith connections:

> *Paddy Murphy went to Mass,*
> *Never missed a Sunday.*
> *Paddy Murphy went to hell,*
> *For what he did on Monday!*

I was once asked to say a few words on the topic, *Do We Still Believe?*, and I had no hesitation in saying that the great majority of Irish people still do. Look, for example, at the full churches on Sunday, the numbers of baptisms, confirmations, and holy communions. People still come to church to have their marriages blessed. We believe, all right.

But the question is: "What is the quality of our faith?" Does it translate into real living? Jesus, in the Gospel of St John, does not say, "Whoever believes in me will never die," but "Whoever *lives* and believes in me will never die" (John 11:26).

It is our whole lives which count, not the hour or half-hour we give, sometimes grudgingly enough, to the Lord at weekend. We must get back to basics. We still believe when we are able to say that we love the Lord—love, not think about—with our whole heart, our whole mind and will, with all our strength.

We still believe when God is the centre of our lives, when there is nothing more important than Him. We still believe when our attitudes, priorities, values, are formed by the Gospel of Jesus Christ. We still believe when we see our Baptism as the most important day of our lives, the day on which we began to live not our own lives, but God's life within us.

Our faith is weak when we are preoccupied with questions such as whether there should or should not be altar girls, or altar boys, for that matter—neither, in fact, is needed in a liturgy properly celebrated—communion in the hand, Eucharistic ministers, etc.

The fundamental question is: "Do you believe in Jesus Christ, and are you always trying to make that belief the centre of all you do and say and are?" If this is not the heart and soul of all our lives and faith and religion, then all the rest is nonsense and we, as the Scriptures put it in a different context, are among the human race the most pitiful of men and women.

Let's put our priorities, as well as our houses, in order!

On Candlemas Day

Some time ago I was visiting a certain house and exchanged the usual greetings on the way in. "How are you doing?" I asked. I didn't mean the question to be taken literally but it was, and I ended up on the receiving end of a litany of laments.

Few escaped. Church and State, priest and prelate, press and politician—all got their share of the stick. Young people, in particular, came in for the severest criticism of all.

It was the closing lines of the lament which stayed with me all that day and for many a day since. For that good soul ended with the poignant remark, "Father, I'm ready to sing my *Nunc Dimittis!*"

The reference, of course, was to the beautiful prayer of Simeon in today's Gospel:

> *Now, Master, you can let your servant go in peace,*
> *just as you promised;*
> *because my eyes have seen the salvation*
> *which you have prepared for all the nations to see,*
> *a light to enlighten the pagans*
> *and the glory of your people Israel.*

The prayer of my friend may have contained the words uttered by Simeon but what a difference in sentiment, in outlook, in hope! One prophesied to the Good News; the other spoke from a valley of darkness, of hopelessness, really.

I know that Mary our Mother will forgive me if on Candlemas Feast I turn the spotlight on two old people, the two old people who met herself and Joseph on that day full of prophecy and promise, the day they journeyed to Jerusalem to present Jesus at the temple.

Simeon was already an old man. Anna's exact age is given in the Gospel account—she was 84 years of age. Both of them, prompted by the Spirit, knew that something full of grace was happening that day, a fateful event, a Person, really, who would be the light and the glory of Israel. And both of them made no bones about talking about this to all who would listen. No one listened more closely than the young Mary and Joseph.

Simeon's words, in particular, must have filled them with worry as well as wonder. For he described the child as destined for the ruin and the resurrection of many in Israel, as a sign of hope for some which would also be rejected by many. He even spoke of a sword piercing Mary's very soul.

Both old people sensed and said that a new age was dawning, an age and a way of life quite different from that in which they grew to old age, were accustomed to, loved and in which they found their way to God. Both were inspired to speak of the new age ushering in light and life, sword and sorrow, ruin and resurrection.

But theirs was no litany of laments but words of hope and encouragement to the newly-married, facing into a new age, as full of worry, perhaps, as of wonder.

It was only when Simeon had given his words of hope and encouragement, of confidence and confirmation that he was able to sing his own great song of joyful release. He had been kept around so many years for this one task. "He would not see death," the Gospel tells us, until he had performed his great final act of ministry, of confirming Mary and Joseph in their faith. None of us, then, has a right to sing or recite Simeon's song unless we, too, are engaged in his ministry of giving hope, of instilling confidence, of saying the word that lightens the load for those they meet along life's road.

God knows—and so do Mary and Joseph—how many days and nights the two of them called to mind the words of Anna and Simeon and mulled over them in the long evenings of their life together. And when Mary's heart was broken in later years, how she must have clung in faith to the Spirit-filled words of Anna and Simeon, spoken so many years before in happier times.

A great number who read those lines are old, over fifty, that is! I wonder how much hope and confidence and confirmation do we instill in young people. How can we expect the young to become "an Easter people whose song is *Alleluia*" if the only song they ever hear from us is "The Way We Were?'

And, indeed, it isn't only the young who need the good word, the kind word. We, all of us, need a ministry of hope and encouragement. Never has there been such a need in our communities and in our country of Annas and Simeons.

I am not saying for one minute that there isn't a great deal wrong with the world we live in. Neither am I saying that all that today's young people say and do is beyond reproach and correction.

I couldn't disagree with the man who wrote:

12

(Some) children today love luxury, They have bad manners, contempt for authority, a dislike for their elders, and they talk instead of work. They contradict their parents, chatter before company, gobble up the best at table and tyrannise their teachers.

But I also notice that these lines weren't written today or yesterday—but 500 years before Christ.

No, I am not looking for an uncritical love for today's young people. What I am praying for on this Candlemas morning, day of light and promise and presentation, what I am pleading for, are more Annas and Simeons who will reach out to the young and the not-so-young with a few words of understanding and love, who will translate, make more sense of life's loneliness and searching and failure.

Pope John Paul, whose love for Mary is an example for all of us, put it this way in one of his last addresses to us in Ireland:

I entrust all this to Mary,
"bright Sun of the Irish race".
May her prayers help all Irish homes
to be like the holy house of Nazareth.
From them may all Christians go forth
as Jesus did from Nazareth.
May they go forth in the power of the Spirit
to continue Christ's work
and to follow in his footsteps
towards the end of the millenium,
into the twenty-first century.
Mary will keep you all close to him
who is "Father of the world to come".
Dia agus Muire libh!
May God and Mary be with you
and with the families of Ireland,
always!

Bored At Mass?

We are all aware of the complaints of some people today about the Mass, that they are "bored" by it. We priests are blamed for poor sermons and poorer liturgies. But I'm afraid that things are not as simple as blaming priests or liturgies. We must look deeper.

The truth is that many Irish Catholic believe that they are doing God a favour by coming to Mass on Sunday and throwing a few shillings and fewer prayers in His direction.

The truth is that a great many people attending Mass on Sundays in our churches spend more time getting ready for a dance or a dinner party than they do getting ready for Mass. The truth is that many spend no time whatsoever in preparation.

The truth is that too often a priest is judged to be a "great man" by the speed by which he can get the people in and out of Mass. The truth is that the only bit of religion the ordinary person gets is listening to the endless debates about the Church's position on this or that subject and, however important such a position is, it is not religion.

Religion is a relationship. Religion is the story, doctrine is the grammar and nothing bores like the word of God made grammar! Religion includes the totality of one's life and one's relationship with God. Doctrine is an attempt to state the essential truths about religion and about our relationship with a Father revealed to us in and through Jesus Christ. Religion is a set of answers a person has to the fundamental questions about the meaning of his or her life.

People complain about the "new liturgy". It is not the liturgy which is faulty but our approach to it.

Christian life is more than liturgy. Liturgy is, indeed, the *principal* way in which we worship God. It was never meant to be the *only* way. When it becomes the *only way*, this asks too much of the liturgy.

At every Mass, for example, we ask the Father to accept this "our sacrifice". We pray that it may be acceptable to Him. But what is *our* sacrifice? What do we bring to the altar every Sunday? A ten penny piece, a fifty pence piece, a pound? What sacrifice do *you* bring with you?

The truth is that those who come with empty hands and empty hearts and empty heads are not in any fit condition to attend Mass.

These will always be bored at Mass. Why come then? To be entertained? To fulfil an obligation? The truth is that far too many Churchgoers are *spectators* at the Sunday Mass when they are called to be *partakers*.

Before the Mass there must come private prayer, prayer offered to the Father in the privacy of one's bedroom.

Before the Mass there must be room in one's life for the Lord in moments of quiet reflection and reading.

Before the Mass there must come sorrow for sin and a firm resolution to put one's life in order.

Before the Mass there must come justice and charity in one's life and forgiveness in one's heart.

Before the Mass there must come a decision to give one's life totally to the Father and a determination to live as Jesus did.

The Mass is mystery not magic. It accomplishes nothing unless it becomes "our sacrifice", joined with that of Christ. Christians are called not to watch the Mass, but to be part of it.

For God's sake stop complaining about the Mass and start doing something before, during and after it.

Altar Servers

I am not writing about this subject because I consider it a matter of great importance, and certainly not the importance given it by those who have made the question of girls serving at the altar a test of allegiance to the Holy See. Just by raising the subject one runs the risk of being accused of the luxury of having nothing more important on one's mind and, when placed alongside the problems and challenges facing society and the Church, the question of altar servers is not one of major significance.

But I have noticed that it is the small issues which at times generate the greatest emotion. Maybe it's because the great tasks facing our age are beyond our capacities and we like to get our hands on more manageable matters. It's also true that certain sections of the media, especially RTE, seem to be attracted to the question of girls serving at the altar. Of course, some of these turn around a few days later and attack the Church for having nothing more important on its agenda!

Anyhow, I have a number of questions and comments to make on the whole question of altar servers in general and girls serving at the altar in particular.

First of all, I endorse the recent recommendation of the US Bishops' document, *One in Christ Jesus: A Pastoral Response to the Concerns of Women for Church and Society*:

> "We support further study of criteria for admission of women to the lay ministries of lector and acolyte. The exclusion of women and girls from certain aspects of service at the altar likewise demands consideration. These instances of exclusion seem to contradict our mandate that women be more visibly involved in the life of the Church."

Secondly, I suggest that one should be able to give reasons why the Church makes a particular law or regulation. To tell a 10-year-old girl that she cannot serve at the altar because the Pope doesn't allow it is good for neither the Pope not the girl in question, not to mention the Church. She will simply ask, "Why doesn't the Pope allow it?" and it's back to square one.

But there is a more fundamental question: what exactly is meant by "altar server" or "serving at the altar"? Is it what a person *does*, or the manner of *dress*, or a person's *proximity* to the altar? Few seem to have noticed that the great majority of altar servers do *nothing* at Mass. For, if the liturgy is properly celebrated, the gifts are brought up to the altar by members of the congregation, and there is no Church law or regulation against girls or women doing so in the Offertory procession. And please don't tell me that women are prevented from ringing the bells!

So, if it's not what the altar server *does*—nothing, for the most part—is it the manner of dress? Personally, I am far from enamoured with the idea of dressing up young girls to look like miniature clerics. Neither, for that matter, am I any more enamoured with the idea of dressing up young boys in a similar manner. In an age when there is so much emphasis on the lay vocation, I would argue for altar servers to be dressed neatly in their own lay clothes.

That leaves us with the matter of the special place close to the altar enjoyed by altar servers, and I, for one, would not fancy the idea of telling a young girl that she must keep a certain distance from the altar. She might remind me, as St Theresa reminded the Lord himself in her prayer, that if women were good enough to stand at the foot of the Cross they are good enough to stand at the foot of the altar!

So, for what they're worth, I offer the following suggestions.

First, if the question of altar servers is to become a divisive one in the Church, then I suggest that we dispense with their services altogether—as we now have them—and have women and men bring up the gifts and prepare the altar at the Offertory of the Mass.

Secondly, I would prefer to see in the entrance procession those who are really doing something during the Mass, for example, the readers, the cantors, the Eucharistic minister where the latter exists, etc.

Thirdly, and directly related to my second point, if we are to continue with the custom of altar servers, I would prefer to see adults serving Mass instead of children.

There is something wrong when young people finish primary school and think that they have grown "too old" for serving Mass. What does this say about the privilege of serving at the altar? That it's for children? On the other hand, imagine the example given if some of our young people's role models were to act as altar servers—for example, a noted athlete or a respected teacher.

I myself served Mass for many years and have the same

emotional attachment to the trade as many thousands of others. But before some of you decide to form a chapter of SAAAB (the Society Against the Abolition of Altar Boys) let us measure our emotional attachments against the very real hurt of a 12-year-old girl who wonders what is wrong with her, or her Church, that she cannot do what her brothers and other boys in her class, are allowed to do.

And please don't tell me that these girls are "radical feminists" or put up to it by mothers who are such. Young girls are asking these questions in parts of our land where they would think that "radical feminism" was the name of a horse running in the Grand National. We had better have answers a little more convincing than, "It's a Church regulation,' or "The Church or the Pope or the bishop or the priest says you can't serve."

We need better reasons than that!

The Easter Gift of Penance

During the Easter season the readings and prayers of the Church speak to us of new life, of hope, of peace, of the Spirit breathing, of healing, of renewal, of reconciliation, of joy, of forgiveness, of power.

Yet our age and our own experience speaks to us of fear, of confusion, of discouragement and despair, of guilt, of hatred, of division, of failure to forgive, of violence, of murder, of greed, of vice, of great sin.

How are we to reconcile the two—the Church's vision and the realities amidst which we live? Or do we even bother to reconcile them? If we don't, then we run the risk of living as if all the prayers and readings we hear in Church at this time of year are so much pie in the sky.

There is one way of reconciling them, not a way, really, but a power. It is called *Penance*: Penance as a virtue and the sacrament of Penance. The Sacrament of Penance is Jesus' Easter gift to the little community which made up His infant Church.

The Sacrament of Penance is the bringing to life of a reality which lies at the very heart of the Church. Take, for example, the opening words of Jesus as He began his public ministry: "The time has come and the kingdom of God is at hand. Repent and believe the Good News."

Again, among His first words after His Resurrection were words instituting the Sacrament of Penance. "Receive the Holy Spirit. Whose sins you shall forgive . . ."

St. Peter, in his great address on Pentecost Sunday, proclaimed: "Repent and let every one of you be baptised in the name of Jesus Christ for the forgiveness of sins."

The Church, in the words of St Ambrose, possesses both water and tears: the water of baptism and the tears of penance.

What has happened to this great power in our lives and in the lives of the Church? Why has the Church become in some places "the Church of six sacraments"?

When one mentions the words "penance" and "confessions", do they bring joy to the hearer, or images of pain and visions of dark secrets whispered in darker corners?

Penance literally means returning home. It should not in the first place be a matter of thinking about one's own needs, problems, sins and fears, but allowing oneself to be caught up into the way of Jesus Christ.

Pope Paul VI reminded us that it is by penance alone that we can approach the kingdom of God, and by penance he meant a profound change of the whole person by which that person begins to consider, judge and arrange his or her life according to the love of God made manifest and given to us in abundance.

The reality is that many people find the recitation of "the same old sins" somewhat unreal. What is needed is a conviction of one's own sinfulness, the conviction which lies at the heart of the man or woman who can cry out, "O God! Be merciful to me, a sinner!"

Surely the Sacrament of Penance must be, in the first place, an encounter with Jesus Christ, who is given to us as a sign of the Father's total love and forgiveness, and as a pledge of grace and strength precisely in those areas of one's life where one has confessed that he or she is broken, wounded, a sinner.

Surely there must be something wrong with our reception of the Sacrament of Penance when we dwell so obsessively on ourselves and our sins that we fail to see Jesus sent to forgive and to reassure. People find the recitation of sins unreal because such a recitation is not linked with a deep desire to change one's way of living.

Penance is gift and virtue and sacrament. It is a coming home over and over again, as often as we stray from a Father who loves us. My Easter-Pentecost prayer for you is that you may rediscover or grow to a greater appreciation of Christ's Easter gift. The Sacrament of Penance is the homeward road to the Prodigal Father.

Hurry home, again and again!

Under A Waterfall of Grace

They had been brought up in the country themselves but had no nostalgia for what they had left behind when they moved to Dublin. It had been a hard enough life and the part of the country in which they were reared was barren and beautiful, a good tourist spot, but you couldn't eat scenery.

They now had a fine house in one of Dublin's more fashionable suburbs. Paul had a good job, and Fionnuala worked part-time in a nearby school. The arrival of the baby, Johnny, was like the last piece of the jigsaw puzzle falling into place. There was great contentment in their lives. They wanted the best for Johnny for whom they had waited so long.

Above all they wanted him to grow up a free child without any of the hang-ups that both of them thought had been part of their lives. They wanted "family" to be something he chose and not a burden landed upon him. For that reason they decided that they would distance themselves from him as much as they could.

Oh, they would look after him all right, but wouldn't smother him with their love. There would be no emotional blackmail in this child's life. No "Daddy" and "Mammy" for Johnny—he would call them Paul and Fionnuala. In the meantime, both of them would be very careful not to try to "buy" his love and affection. Their relationship with Johnny would be proper. It would be up to him, in time to come, how that relationship would develop.

The same applied to all of their relationships, their likes and dislikes. Paul would not bring him to the rugby games when he was old enough to go; Fionnuala would not bring him to visit her mother's. He would not be baptised into any church. He could chose all this for himself later when he was the right age.

I need say no more. Paul and Fionnuala's "experiment" was doomed from the start. It had all been tried before, even to the point of putting a baby into a box! There is no way a child can be protected from the world into which he is born. The child's world is the world of the adults who brought him into life without consulting him in the first place.

Why go to such extremes in attempting not to impose their ways upon him when they imposed their way on him in relation to the most fundamental question of all, namely, whether he wanted to be born? He has no freedom then. There had been no consultation with him on that occasion.

You will, I hope, think that the situation I have described above is far-fetched and fanciful. It is. As far-fetched and fanciful as those parents who call themselves Christian and who try to bring their children up in a neutral, value-free world, fearful less they impose their beliefs on their children.

It is far-fetched and fanciful because no one should grow up without love and relationships, without experiencing what it is to live in a community with certain values and beliefs. How, for example, could a father and mother deny love to a child of theirs for 17 years in the belief that by loving a child they are somehow diminishing his freedom?

How, too, can a Christian parent bring up a child without telling him of his or her other Father, without bringing him into the warmth of the Christian family, without making him aware of his relationships and relatives?

There are some who believe it is fashionable to bring Johnny up in the womb of the world but, in matters relating to his heavenly Father, to put him into an isolation ward until he can, at some later date, decide for or against God. How infinitely sad! What a deprivation!

So unlike that other little Johnny whose baptism John O'Shea celebrated in his *Prayer at a Baptism:*

> *You came among us*
> *in a new womb of blankets . . .*
> *We did rites over you*
> *with all the ceremony of a primitive tribe*
> *painting their babies . . .*
> *Your parents held you*
> *under a waterfall of grace*
> *and your sleeping eyes*
> *suddenly sat up and stared*
> *into the funny faces of our love . . .*
>
> *Afterwards*
> *you slept*
> *and we ate and drank and laughed*
> *and knew*
> *our love would outlast diamonds.*

The Real Meaning of Confirmation

No one was able to give the bishop an example of how moral courage, one of the gifts of the Holy Spirit received at Confirmation, might appear in the life of the newly confirmed, and so he decided to give one himself.

"Suppose," he began, "an entire group of little scouts was camping out overnight and it came to bedtime. Ninety-nine of the little fellows jumped into bed without saying night prayers, but one little scout knelt down on his bed and said his prayers as usual. That, my dear children, would be an example of moral courage. Now, could any of you give me an example of your own?"

"Yes, my Lord," volunteered one little lad. "Suppose there were one hundred little bishops on an overnight trip and when it came to bedtime, ninety-nine of them knelt down by their bedsides and said their prayers as usual, but one little bishop jumped into bed without saying any. That, my Lord, would be an example of moral courage!"

For a bishop, the seasons of the turning year include the season of Confirmation. It's a good time, a happy time. At least for the majority. It's also a fairly busy time.

Children have to be prepared. Parents are asked to attend pre-Confirmation meetings. As one wag put it recently, "There are so many meetings to attend these days. There are pre-Baptism, pre-First Confession, pre-First Communion, pre-Confirmation, and pre-Marriage courses. When are they going to come up with a pre-death one?" Don't worry, they're on the way!

Seriously, the amount of preparation for the sacraments is as welcome as it is impressive. These courses, the dedication of the teachers in preparing the children, the care with which the liturgy is prepared, the amount of books, audio and video tapes and other resource material available are all very encouraging.

Not so encouraging is the entry of good "Mr Consumerism" into the field in the form of advertisements in the various media for First Communion and Confirmation dresses. No one will deny young people the joy of their big day, but some of the style, including a visit to the hairdresser, for example, is "over the top", especially when it puts an impossible financial burden on already hard-pressed parents.

Likewise, it is good to see the whole family get together for a meal afterwards where the poor mother is waited on for a change, but the emphasis should be on simplicity in dress, and in all the celebrations. Young people shouldn't end up in a pub on the day of their Confirmation, and the notion of the day ending with a disco for the newly anointed is sad, indeed. Everything in moderation except moderation!

Is it old age coming over me? Am I becoming old-fashioned? Am I scolding or just plain giving out? I hope not. After all, Confirmation is the celebration of the mystery of the coming of God's Holy Spirit into the lives of the young, and there should be simplicity and reverence and awe not only in everything surrounding the liturgy but also in the celebrations afterwards.

It would be sad indeed to see Confirmation Day become like those wedding days where all the fuss over the hotel bookings, honeymoon arrangements, floral decorations, bridesmaid's dresses and photographs etc. have succeeded in pushing into the background the central reality of the Lord's making a covenant for eternity with two newly-weds.

But back to Confirmation. I have attended many a Confirmation where the candidates for the Sacrament were beautifully turned out in their school uniforms. There was minimal expenditure on photographs, there was a beautiful simplicity about the whole day, and one could feel the Spirit shining through.

Irish parents, in their great love for their children, want to do the very best for them. But surely "the very best" would be to keep their children's eyes and minds and hearts on the central reality of the day: the advent of the Spirit of God into their young hearts.

Above all, I don't think that going into debt is a particularly sensible way to celebrate the reception of a sacrament of peace and joy and love. There has to be a happy medium between being a Scrooge, on the one hand, and letting the whole celebrations get out of harmony with the reality of what the day is all about.

To understand what is happening at Confirmation, it is important to watch carefully for the signs under which lie the great mysteries which are happening in the lives of the young people.

First of all, there is "the standing up for the faith" of the young people to renew their Baptismal promises, or rather to profess publicly for the first time and in their own name the promises made on their behalf on the day of their Baptism by their parents and godparents.

Next, there is the imposing of hands and the prayer. The outstretched hands are always a sign of the giving of gifts, in this instance the gifts of the Spirit of God. To confirm this giving of gifts—hence the name "Confirmation"—the young people are now anointed with chrism, the perfumed oil of God's anointing. They are now "chrismed", and since to be Christ means to be the "Chrismed" or to be the "Anointed One", we have many new "Christs" or "anointed ones" on Confirmation Day.

So keep your eyes open during the season of Confirmation. Each springtime our towns and countrysides are made beautiful with a myriad of nature's flowers. More wonderful still, they are graced with thousands of God's young anointed. What a blessed and happy people we are if only we had eyes to see!

A Question of Faith

A certain man was walking near the edge of a cliff one summer's day when the whole pathway caved in and sent him hurtling down towards the sea a thousand feet below. Desparately he reached out for something to hold on to in an effort to break his fall and, as luck would have it, he grabbed a sapling growing on the cliff-side.

Looking down on the waves crashing over the rocks below, gazing at the sheer surface of the cliff, and realising how precarious was his grip on the sapling tree, he cried out to God for help.

To his great surprise, a loud voice from heaven answered; "I am the Lord whom you have called upon for help. Do you truly believe in me?"

"With all my heart," replied the terrified supplicant.

"Do you truly love me?" questioned the voice from above.

"With all my heart," came the reply.

"If you truly believe in me, and truly love me," spoke the Lord, "then let go of that branch you are holding!"

Terrified, the man looked at the rock and sea below, at the heavens above, at the tree he was holding on to and at the roots which were beginning to part company with the cliff.

Minutes of the most awful agony of indecision passed before the man looked heavenward again, before addressing one last plaintive cry in the direction of the voice: "Is there anybody else up there I can talk to?"

What is the Spiritual Life?

The difficulty in speaking about the spiritual life is that the spiritual life can be made to appear as something apart from life itself, that spirituality is some section of a person's life which one works at when one is at prayer just as one works at another part of life when one plays golf, another when one goes on holidays, and so on.

Authentic spirituality is not about the practice of spiritual exercises only but is about reducing to unity, or integrating, the programme of one's external activity and one's interior life. Or to put it another way, he is genuinely a spiritual man, a holy man, who possesses a certain wholeness or integrity in his life. Holiness is not about doing more and doing it better, but about being a certain type of person, a person whose life has a definite direction, a goal, a unity of purpose about it.

Spirituality, then, is first of all about integrating one's life and centring it on a goal, on someone or something. Integrity demands an answer to the question: who or what is the central name one carries in one's heart and which gives purpose and direction to one's whole life?

"I don't know Who—or What—put the question," wrote Dag Hammarskjold in *Markings*. "I don't know when it was put. I don't even remember answering. But at some moment I did answer *Yes* to Someone—or Something—and from that hour I was certain that existence is meaningful and that, therefore, my life, in self-surrender, had a goal". St Paul put it much more simply: "Life to me, of course, is Christ!" Both were speaking of their lives and of what and who gave meaning to those lives.

The Scriptural exhortation to be "perfect as your Heavenly Father is perfect" is not, in the first instance at any rate, a moral exhortation to improve one's conduct by ever greater effort. It is primarily a call to conversion, to be wholly turned, with the whole will and being, to God as he is turned to us.

It is a response of obedience and of faith. One is called to act with a certain purpose or meaning or end in view, with a single-mindedness. A person is to become "one-eyed", as the early Christians were described, from the analogy of the archer closing one eye so that his visual concentration might be totally on the target.

St Paul uses similar analogies of the runner and the fighter. "All the runners at the stadium are trying to win, but only one of them gets the prize. You must run in the same way, meaning to win. All the fighters at the game go into strict training; they do this just to win a wreath that will wither away, but we do it for a wreath that will never wither. That is how I run, intent on winning; that is how I fight, not beating the air." (1 Cor.9:24-26).

There is one very real danger in all of this and that is the assumption that prayer is being down-played and that there is place for nothing but work. Nothing could be further from the truth. Quite simply, one's life will never become a source of holiness if the Lord is not sought out in prayer. Periods of prayer are privileged moments in which we withdraw, not to engage in any flight from the world but to discover the Lord at the heart of one's life. It is principally in prayer that we will be able to see and create an expectancy for meeting in "the bits and pieces of everyday" the Lord of our life.

More and more in today's busy world we need to pray—all types of prayer: prayer on one's knees and prayer on the run, vocal prayer and mental prayer, prayer with people and prayer for people. And when one is unable to pray, one should at least say his prayers! The disciple is not greater than the Master and the Master frequently stole away from people to go to places of beauty and quiet, to be by himself and with the Father. Precisely because our secular environment offers us so few spiritual aids, we must develop our own disciplines, our own structures.

Years ago at a diocesan priests' retreat in Ossory, when Fr Jack Dalrymple spoke of the need for priests to make substantial investment of their time in prayer, a retreatant protested, "But, Father Jack, from the time I get up in the morning to the time I go to bed at night, I simply don't have that kind of time."

To which Fr Dalrymple replied, "Perhaps, Father, but what about from the time you go to bed at night to the time you get up in the morning!"

Shortly before he died, the same Fr Dalrymple, a Scottish diocesan priest, wrote:

> I have always been insistent on the need for prayer, deep contemplative prayer, in my life and have tried to practise it. In practice in my present life this means that I get up every morning at 6.30 and pray till 8.00 when I get myself some

breakfast, but in earlier times as a priest I have prayed for as much as four hours a day and have seen that as necessary for me. As a result of this prayer I have felt called to exercise my priesthood in a certain way.

"As a result of this prayer I have felt called to exercise my priesthood in a certain way." What better way to describe a spirituality marked by integrity? And all God's people are similarly challenged.

Why Don't You Excommunicate The Terrorists?

The whole question of violence in Northern Ireland is one about which I receive many a letter, many of them complaining that the Bishops do not take a strong enough stand against IRA violence. The question as to why the Bishops do not excommunicate members of the IRA also comes up from time to time.

First of all, could I say that there is no item which appears more frequently on the agenda of meetings of the Irish Bishops' Conference than violence in our country. Over the years it has been the policy of the Bishops to issue a condemnation of every incident of serious violence, particularly when there has been loss of life.

Generally it is the Bishop of the diocese where the violence has been perpetrated who issues such a statement. On other occasions formal condemnations of violence are issued by the Conference of Bishops. The number of statements issued in a particular year constitute an extensive record of the Bishops' condemnation of violence and of their appeal for justice, reconciliation and peace in Northern Ireland. Unfortunately these statements are not always carried by the media.

The teaching of the Catholic Church in Ireland in regard to the violence of the IRA is clear and unequivocal. The Bishops, especially those in the North, have on hundreds of occasions denounced various murders, attempted murders, kidnappings, destruction of property carried out by the IRA and other organisations.

They have condemned membership of these organisations as sinful and have called on their people to give no assistance, support or approval of any kind to them or to their supporters. Their words have in many instances been ignored by those who have long since given up the practice of their faith as Catholics. It is hard to see how excommunication would add anything to this.

In regard to excommunication of people involved in paramilitary violence, the Bishops have made a judgement regarding the likely effects of imposing excommunication on members of the IRA who profess to be Catholics. When excommunication was invoked in Ireland in the 1920's, it proved ineffective as a moral sanction.

It also alienated many good Catholics, themselves strongly opposed to violence, because of the widespread belief that it was being imposed as a political rather than a spiritual discipline. The Catholic Church in Ireland, therefore, has had historical experience of excommunication and it has not been a happy one.

Excommunication for moral offences is a spiritual penalty intended to reform hearts and minds. But, for those who have not listened to the constant pleas of the Bishops and even of the Pope, excommunication is certainly unlikely to be a more effective means of achieving conversion.

It could easily bring the Church's discipline into disrepute by being flaunted as a "badge of merit' by apologists for the paramilitaries. Although excommunication is a penalty intended to bring people to a spiritual reconciliation, it would inevitably be interpreted in a political sense here. Whatever good it might conceivably achieve would be smothered in political argument and propaganda.

However, the fact is that by choosing to ignore the clear teaching of the Church on a matter so grave, those who willingly participate in the acts of murder and violence do in a very real sense—though not in the canonical sense—excommunicate themselves.

There is one further consideration in this situation. Most of the excommunications in the former Code of Canon Law have been removed from the new Code of Canon Law which came into effect in 1983. The emphasis on the Church's role of reconciliation would in fact suggest a call to repentance for sin rather than a rejection of the sinner.

What I'd Tell The Pope

What would you say to the Pope if you had his ear for twenty minutes? Believe it or not there is a whole book written on the theme. In it several Americans contribute their "priorities for the Church" as they're called.

They would talk to him about the ordination of women, married priests, divorce, the role of women in the Church, authority, basic Christian communities, ecumenism, mixed marriages, seminary formation, laity in the Church. You name it. They'd talk about it!

Well, I had the Pope's ear for twenty minutes and he asked me a few things and I talked to him about a few things. But he communicated to me more by what he didn't say. "Body language" I think they call it!

Each bishop, on his official visit to Rome, has twenty minutes or thereabouts with the Pope. At the end of my allotted time a little buzzer went off and a photographer came in. The Pope, I remember, gestured rather wearily in the direction of the buzzer as much as to say, "My time is not my own!"

It was then that I knew what I would say when I am given, if I am given, another twenty minutes. I think I'll just say, "Listen, Pope John Paul, you must be tired sitting here morning after morning looking at strange people from foreign lands coming in to see you and to speak with you and to ask you questions or give you advice. Why don't you just sit over there in the corner and put your feet up and rest yourself!" In that way I think I would be making a significant contribution to the Church and to the Pope.

Or maybe I'd pick up the courage to say to him, "Could you and I pray for the diocese of Ferns, for the young and the old, the priests and the religious, the sick and the lonely, all those people who have your picture hanging in their homes and who love you very much and who want me to tell you that they do? Could we pray together for your ministry and mine?"

Or if that mightn't be acceptable to the Pope, I could say to him: "Holy Father, I don't know about you, but I'm tired of talking and writing, and reading and arguing. I'm tired of rows and fights and controversies. I've really had it with people telling me what I'm doing wrong and of how great they are and how they know what's wrong with the Church and you and me and the priests and the teachers and the schools and the catechists. Would you mind telling me what you think is the most important thing in the life of the Church, in your life, in my life?"

Did it ever occur to those, who were invited to give to the world the message of what they would say to the Pope, to ask themselves: "Do I really have anything of any great and world-shaking significance to say to this good man that he doesn't already know or has heard a thousand times from a thousand other people far holier and far more intelligent than I?"

Would it ever occur to them to say nothing, to sit silently in the Pope's presence and ask him for a word of wisdom, of encouragement—a word for life?

These thoughts occurred to me when I was reading recently the story of the Samaritan woman and Jesus at the well. She might not have known who He was but she must have suspected that He was someone very special. Now was her big moment, the chance of a lifetime. She would never have an opportunity like this again.

Here she was and He knew well the type of woman she was and something was expected from Him. After all, it was a disgrace and a scandal that He was even speaking with her at all. He was a Jew. She was a Samaritan. Jews didn't speak with Samaritans.

Who spoke first? He did. What did He say? "Would you please give me a drink of water!" Now that's getting your priorities right.

"We Are Going Down"

If God grants me the blessing of another visit to the Holy Land, I would dearly love to spend more time by the Sea of Galilee. In particular, I would like to get a boat, row out on the lake and just sit there and think. Not so much think as imagine. I would like the space and the time and the quiet to go back in my mind's eye to the many incidents in the life of the Person I love which occurred on and around this holy water.

Jesus loved Galilee. He loved to escape from the hustle and bustle, the business and politics of the big city. He loved to wake early and go down to the places overlooking the lake, to be swept up into its peace and beauty, its storms and churnings, to see on its calm face and in its mighty stirrings the face of His beloved Father.

He would return refreshed to His friends to share with them His thoughts, His prayers, His love. Above all, He would share with them His Father. He wasn't too successful, and this annoyed Him. Really annoyed Him. Of that he left them in no doubt on more than one occasion.

One of those occasions was on that very lake. It was the "coming-of-evening" time of day and Jesus wanted to cross over to the other side of the lake. The lake is notorious for its sudden and very dangerous squalls and when waves started breaking into the boat, the friends of Jesus panicked. Jesus slept.

"Master, do you not care? We are going down!" was the message they gave Him as they shook Him awake.

And He woke up and rebuked the wind and said to the sea: "Quiet now! Be calm!" And the wind dropped, and all was calm again.

Then He said to them: "Why are you so fightened? How is it that you have no faith?"

They were filled with awe and said to one another: "Who can this be? Even the wind and the sea obey Him."

On Galilee I thought about that incident. The storm rising, Jesus sleeping, the disciples breaking out into a sweat of alarm and fear, accusing Jesus of not caring, predicting doom and gloom—"We are going down!" I want to think about it again, to let sink into my heart the image of Jesus, in the heart of the storm, speaking to the wind: "Quiet now! Be calm!"

I want to reflect more on the rebuke addressed to the disciples by Jesus: "How is it that you have no faith?" And the disciples' awful confession or profession of faith in Him whom even the wind and the sea obey.

I long to be part of this ongoing story today, for in today's Church there are many whose message is, "We are going down!" Or rather, and worse still, "We are going down if you don't do what I tell you!" There are those among us who would even rebuke Jesus for sleeping while they alone keep Peter's boat afloat.

"Keep your eyes on us, and you will be safe!" they tell us. Personally, I intend to keep my eyes on Jesus, confess my lack of faith, and pray with that good man in Sacred Scripture: "Lord Jesus, I believe. Help the little faith that I have!"

Who's Stopping You?

A quarter of a century after the Second Vatican Council there is still a great need for precision when we come to the question of involvement of laity in the Church. If the priest is not careful, such talk can result in the laity meeting to decide what the priest should or should not be doing.

If the lay people aren't careful, the end product may be the introduction of a more subtle form of clericalisation in the Church. That is, the lay calling will be defined in terms of assisting the priest.

Secondly, there is the mistaken notion that action takes place at the level of the National Conference of Bishops. At times it seems that every group in the country is trying to get a meeting with the Conference of Bishops. I am long enough a bishop to know that, whatever about the Conference's being a likely place to mull over ideas and strategies, it is at the local level of diocese or deanery or parish that the real action takes place.

Thirdly, there appears to be considerable anger among certain sections of the laity, particularly women, because of their perception of inequality within the Church. Anger and perceptions of injustice and inequality are very real and must be addressed. They are, however, not strategies—and strategies are what are most urgently needed today. Strategies and models.

First of all, when it comes to involving the laity in the Church, there is nothing more important than getting the theory right. There is nothing as practical as a good theory. What exactly does involvement of the laity mean? What is the essence of the lay vocation?

Get that wrong and the whole project is doomed. A married couple told me recently of their involvement in prayer groups, in study groups, in service groups, only to discover that their own children were running wild and stumbling from one crisis to another. What is the sense of devoting time to involvement in the Church when such involvement takes from "the domestic church" which is the home? Surely there is something very wrong with that type of involvement?

Involvement in the Church is not in the first place a matter of helping the priest. It is certainly not a matter of replacing the priest.

Some serious study should be devoted to what exactly it is. Pope Paul's *Evangelization Today* would be an excellent starting point in such an examination.

Secondly, the various vocations must come together to examine how each of their callings contributes to the building up of the Body of Christ which is the Church. Blueprints are fine but they must take into account the landscape, and only the locals know the landscape. The theory must be owned by the locals and applied by the locals. Otherwise the plant will wither sooner or later, mostly sooner.

What all this means above everything else is structures. Yes, structures. Structures aren't "in" these days and perhaps that's why we have more talk than action. There is no scarcity of talkers, but the real movers in Ireland today are the people who prepare for meetings, know what they want done, attend meetings, and get things done at meetings and after meetings.

Let's face it. There are those who speak passionately about change, who write emotively about not having a say in the life of the parish. Yet, when a meeting is called to do something about this, these people will not attend. Paradoxically, the attendance at such a meeting, which has been called to discuss changes to facilitate greater participation in the life of the parish, is made up almost entirely of people who were quite happy with things the way they were.

Of course, part of the problem can also be the nature of meetings, namely, they are ill-prepared and disastrously conducted. There is great need, therefore, for a training in the basic skills of how to conduct meetings.

If history tells us anything, it speaks of results accomplished by those who are committed to a certain goal, who operate according to a set plan, who have very clear structures to guide them and hold them accountable.

The great dream of the round-table Church at which all the gifts of the Holy Spirit are recognised and given full scope will take some clear thinking, hard planning, training in skills, creating of suitable structures, and above all else the commitment of some doers.

It is time to move beyond anger and alienation. It is time to answer as sincerely as we can: "Who is really holding me back?"

Moses and His Ten Suggestions

It is easy enough to pray for the kingdom of God to come on earth. We do it every time we say the *Our Father*. It's not that difficult to preach about the need for lay people to promote God's kingdom of justice and peace in the bits and pieces of their everyday life. We priests do that all the time. It's expected of us.

It's quite another matter to get down to specifics and give practical advice on how, for example, a merchant banker who is a Christian attempts to realise God's kingdom in his profession. Or a television star.

So when such lay people speak out, I listen with increased interest and attention. Not so long ago two prominent people, one a banker, one a television star, spoke out quite clearly and forcefully on the subjects of honesty in banking and personal morality. Your interest, I hope, will not be lessened by the fact that both are Americans.

We usually hear only about the daft things happening in America. We seldom hear of the vibrancy of the life of faith, and the genuine search for Christian truth and its promotion amidst what is too glibly called "secular' reality. These two men give sound advice.

James O'Donnell is an investment banker in New York. Recently he wrote a short piece in the journal, *America*. His advice sounded eminently sound to me. In effect, Mr. O'Donnell was advising young people to think of their future employment or profession in terms of what they are good at doing right now.

What do you like to spend your time doing at present? Where does your attention drift when you are doing nothing in particular? Is there a profession in that line? There may not be as much money, but there may be considerably more happiness.

O'Donnell goes further and talks to young people about something he admits may cause them to yawn or laugh: the need to develop a healthy respect for temptation. He does not apologise.

> Sin and temptation are very real forces in the workplace, and we had all better stop trying to ignore or trivialise them. The

temptation that faces me in my business, which is that of managing money, and in my life is the temptation to serve myself before and above everything else.

We laugh at the notions of sin and temptation because we think that the devils of this world live in hell and run round in red tights and carry pitchforks. But as Alexander Solzhenitsyn said, "The line separating good from evil passes through the heart of every human being." Face it: We are all capable of becoming devils.

Mr O'Donnell gives us an identikit of a devil which tempts a lot of young people in choosing a particular career. These devils are usually very well dressed, belong to the right clubs, know all the right things to say and the right places to eat. Many of them, however, are quite devoid of any ability to distinguish right from wrong or of any ability to see that others do not exist merely to serve them or the system of which they are a part. They think of others simply as obstacles to be moved or conquered.

And a last piece of advice to those choosing a career from this senior bank vice-president: Don't think that the high-paid job is the one that will make you most happy. That mistake could cost you dearly. Your life is far more than your career, even though the contrary may seem to be true today.

Ted Koppel is America's answer to Gay Byrne! He has his own late, late show on America's ABC Television. It is called *Nightline*. It's extremely popular, and it's watched by millions of Americans. Mr Koppel gave an address recently at the prestigious Duke University in Durham, North Carolina.

No more than Gay Byrne, one wouldn't accuse Ted Koppel of being in the employ of the churches! Nor, as they say in America, is he "into" religion. Yet he chose to deliver this compelling message to his young audience.

Americans, he told the Class of '87, have actually convinced themselves that slogans will save them. Shoot up if you must, but use a clean needle. Enjoy sex whenever and with whomever you wish, but wear a condom.

No! The answer is no. Not because it isn't cool or smart or because you might end up in jail or dying in an Aids ward, but no because it's wrong, because we have spent 5,000 years as a race of rational human beings, trying to drag ourselves out of the primeval slime by searching for truth and moral absolutes.

In its purest form, truth is not a polite tap on the shoulder. It is a howling reproach. What Moses brought down from Mount Sinai were not the Ten Suggestions.

Koppel's remarks about the Ten Commandments are reminiscent of those of Soren Kierkegaard on the same topic: "Most people really believe that the Christian commandments are intentionally a little too severe—like putting the clock ahead half an hour to be sure of not being late in the morning."

Isn't the Holy Spirit working in powerful ways, showing up in unusual places such as a New York investment bank and an American television station!

Lord, may Your Kingdom come!

In Praise of Marriage

If you were asked the question, "What is the central word of revelation?", how would you answer? Confronted with this question John Paul II has no hesitation in replying: "God loves his people."

Moreover he sees this "central word" proclaimed through the living and concrete word whereby a man and a woman express their conjugal love. "Their bond of love becomes the image and the symbol of the covenant which unites God and his people."

In an age in which there is so much controversy surrounding marriage and the family it is vitally important to understand Christian marriage as a proclamation of the central word of revelation, of the central Gospel truth that God loves his people.

There is no need to be on the defensive all the time. People who possess the Gospel of Jesus Christ must come out of the "Upper Room" of their fear and share the good news with others.

I sometimes think that the Holy Spirit on that first Pentecost morning did not settle for putting little tongues of flames *over* the heads of the followers of Jesus whom fear had locked into the Cenacle in Jerusalem, the birthplace of the Church.

I suspect the Spirit put a little fire *under* them, transforming them from a fearful bunch into a vibrant community who nearly knocked one another down to get through the previously locked doors and out into the streets to tell everyone who would listen of Jesus Christ and the wonders he had done in their lives!

Jesus Christ and the Gospel of Jesus Christ do not need to be defended—they need to be proclaimed. Likewise, Christian marriage and the family need in the first place and above all else to be proclaimed. I am not saying that Christian marriage and the family do not need to be defended—they do.

But the proclamation of marriage and the family as the central word of revelation, the good news that God loves his people, must always be the context in which any defence is made. This good news, this gospel of marriage and the family, needs to be shouted from the roof-tops of the world.

I have often said what I thought should be very obvious to anyone: there are many excellent marriages, happy homes, loving parents and grateful children.

Men and women still do love one another. Young people still dream and hope that their love will be different—and it will; that their marriages will be unique—and they will. I expressed my conviction that the heart of marriage is still sound.

It is sometimes necessary to state the obvious, to repeat again and again the good news, for if we continue to hear only of broken marriages, child abuse, wife beating, unfaithful spouses, we might tend to overlook the truth that all of these things, though far too numerous, are still the exception.

It is not a criticism of the media to say that these things make the headlines. They make the headlines because they are the exception. Happy marriages are not kept out of the papers because of any perversity on the part of the media; they are excluded because they are in no way out of the ordinary. What an extraordinary thing it would be to read as a headline in one of our national dailies: DUBLIN COUPLE HAPPILY MARRIED FOR FOUR YEARS.

Yet, when I made this point in the past, I was accused of ignoring the tragedy of marriage breakdowns, the horrors of child abuse, the obscenity of spouse beating. I did no such thing.

But I do believe that to focus constantly and almost exclusively on failure and breakdown is as effective a way to undermine the institution of marriage as some of the more obvious efforts made to accomplish the same objective.

Those who uphold marriage and the family must bear in mind this danger also. They, too, can become totally preoccupied with the difficulties facing marriage and the family in modern times. There is the very real danger of forgetting that the family is founded on God himself—is, in fact, an expression of His love.

The power of the family to survive is enormous. It would be difficult to exaggerate its resilience. It has survived wars and concentration camps, famines and plagues. It has weathered the direct frontal attack of hostile ideologies and naked State aggression.

Again, I say, marriage and the family needs to be proclaimed as much or more than they need to be defended. What we need most today is the Christian vision of marriage captured and lived out by couples, a vision which will capture the imagination and hearts of all, especially the young.

Pope John Paul II specifically challenges married people to do just this, reminding them that Christ has made them witnesses and given them an understanding of the faith and the grace of speech so that the power of the Gospel might shine forth in their daily social and family life:

> Christian spouses and parents can and should offer their unique and irreplaceable contribution to the elaboration of an authentic evangelical discernment in the various situations and cultures in which men and women live their marriage and their family life. They are qualified for this role by their charism or specific gift, the gift of the sacrament of matrimony. (*On the Family*).

What the Church and society in Ireland need is precisely this "unique and irreplaceable" contribution. In the long run, this will prove to be the best defence of marriage and the family.

All in the Family

A colleague of mine tells the story of addressing a parents' group in Dublin. Realising that parents can be fairly reticent about taking part in a discussion, he used a short video production designed to get them talking.

The mini-film showed a father returning from work one evening and doing all the things a father isn't supposed to do.

He mutters a greeting to his wife, slumps down to read the evening paper, continues to read the same paper at the dinner table, has a row with his daughter over "that long-haired lout you are going out with", roars at his son for even thinking about borrowing his car—all the time asking his wife to fetch him this or that.

The film ended and my colleague invited comments on it from the audience. It worked: several hands were in the air.

But no one surpassed the first gentleman's contribution: "That piece of film has pointed out exactly what I've been telling the wife and children for years. No one bothers to say grace before or after meals any more!"

We all laugh at this modern "Archie Bunker" type because we see glimpses of our own blind spots in him. There are "credibility gaps" in all our lives.

Parents, however, have an additional problem—children! There are in Ireland today no keener critics, no sharper observers of human conduct, than children.

Their extremely sensitive antennae are forever finely tuned to pick up any and all signals of "credibility gaps" in the lives and conduct of their parents and elders.

This is one reason why example is so important. Paul VI reminded us on more than one occasion that young people no longer listen to parents. (And we could all add: teachers, priests, bishops.) They listen to witnesses only, the Pope concluded.

That is why youth's heroes and heroines are people who are living witnesses or examples of what they profess. Young people expect us all to live up to the standards of a Mother Teresa or an Archbishop Romero.

Parents, however, live in day-to-day contact with their children. I suspect that, if a Mother Teresa or an Archbishop Romero were to live in such proximity, some credibility gaps would soon be observed by keen young eyes and ears. Of course they would. Otherwise, we would have no real-life saints, merely plastic ones.

It would be a great mistake, however, if all the example, all the credibility, is demanded from one side in the relationship. Parents, priests and others who have the responsibility of forming young people in the Christian faith should challenge them to put their faith into practice.

I accept the argument that youth must first be attracted before they are preached to, but there is always a danger that we might end up entertaining them rather than challenging them.

The writer Andrew Greeley described "Greeley's law" as follows: what the Catholic Church forgets, other people and groups discover! When we stopped asking people to fast for a few hours, for example, all sorts of organisations began to challenge them to fast for 24 or 48 hours.

Everytime I see fund-raising college students pushing a piano or a bed or some other such object along one of our main roads, I always think of them as modern-day pilgrims.

I suspect that the challenge they present to young people is one of the features which attract European youth in their thousands each year to the monks at Taize in France.

Taize places great trust in young people. It also directly challenges them.

For example, in the area of prayer, parents can learn a great deal from Brother Roger's talks to young people. He continually challenges them to create small signs of prayer in the midst of human life.

Such a sign of prayer and contemplation is a place where our joys and hopes are set before God, where we entrust to the Lord our own sadness and worries and those of others. It is a place where we welcome God in confident trust.

Suppose we prepared ourselves to find ways for our home to become a little centre of contemplation?

What if we let old people also take part in this search, so that their homes too could become places to welcome God and their life could find new meaning?

And what if children prepared a corner for prayer, with an icon, and with the Bible open to the text of the day? And if they invited their families to come once a week and kneel down for a prayer, even in silence, without words, a simple prayer to ask God for forgiveness and to forgive one another?

Notice the challenge: the adults are to be allowed to take part in the search for a way to make the home a little centre of contemplation.

Won't you try it sometime soon? Won't you look for ways to challenge your children to a more lively faith, a more responsible faith?

Television and the Family

One of the longest running debates in modern times has been about the effect of television-viewing on people, in general, and children, in particular. In the USA the National Institute of Mental Health, under the auspices of the Surgeon General, published in 1972 a report which found a close link between televised violence and later aggressive behaviour in children.

In 1982 this report was updated, presenting a comprehensive review of the many studies that has been published since 1972. Its major conclusion was to confirm the relationship between televised violence and later aggressive behaviour.

The later report also noted that television could no longer be viewed as mere entertainment: it has an important part to play in the total process of child development.

In general the television industry did not accept the findings. Indeed one of the larger networks published a brochure purporting to demonstrate "serious flaws" in the report. The Surgeon General criticised this brochure, calling it "an embarrassment to the social-science research community as well as to the media".

Now one of the seven outside scientific advisers to the National Institute of Mental Health, Eli Rubinstein, a research professor of mass communications, in a speech given at Catholic University of America, has posed three questions:

- How has the family been portrayed on television?

- How have these portrayals influenced the family?

- What can be done to increase the constructive impact of television on the family and the constructive impact of the family on television?

Professor Rubinstein's answer to the first question is that if you want to find models for healthy creative family life, television provides rather few examples. In defence of the television industry he is quick to point out, however, that television is in the business of selling products and not of improving family living!

The dilemma is that in selling products they also sell images of family life. A goal that is yet to be realised would be to better reconcile the pressure to deliver an audience to the commercial with the need to serve that audience more constructively between commercials.

Two serious negative consequences arise from the amount of time spent watching television, an average of seven hours per day!

Firstly, television has a serious impact because of the behaviour it presents, merely by the sheer use of time that might otherwise be devoted to other pursuits.

Secondly, where parents participate and encourage the children to participate, for example, by discussing with their children what they have seen on television, the negative effects of televised violence can be mitigated and the positive effects can be enhanced.

In studies done in the late 1970's it was discovered that what was called "post-viewing discussion" by trained group leaders tended to reduce the effects of watching televised violence among youngsters in an institution for disturbed children.

Other researchers have found the same beneficial effects when parents in normal households use television viewing as a stimulus for parent-child interaction.

What are some of the practical implications of all of this research?

Firstly, it is just as wrong and as simplistic for us to put all the responsibility on the television industry as it is for network executives to say that parents can just turn the television off if the amount of viewing by their children is excessive.

Secondly, there doesn't seem to be any simple external control solution. Professor Rubinstein considers gadgets such as electronic locking devices on television sets a poor substitute for active parental involvement.

Thirdly, public-action groups have an important place in educating parents, in admonishing the industry and in goading the government to fulfil their respective responsibilities.

Fourthly, the government is faulted for being much less productive than it could have been. On a more positive note, Professor Rubinstein cites a bill pending in Congress which calls for the broadcast each weekday of a minimum of one hour per day of programming specifically designed to enhance the education of children.

The industry itself must clearly realise that its treatment of the young viewers has primarily been one of exploitation and not one of careful attention to the needs of this vulnerable segment of the viewing public.

It must accept the overwhelming body of research that confirms the significant role television plays as an influence on the social and psychological aspects of child development.

Dr. Rubinstein writes:

> It baffles me that the industry can recognise and accept that role—and spend millions of dollars to enhance that impact—and simultaneously deny that it influences children who spend so many of their waking hours in front of the television set.

At the same time parents must also accept and vigorously address their own responsibilities on how their children use television. There is, Dr Rubinstein thinks, a healthy growth in parental involvement but it needs much more participation, especially among the many families whose television is either still used as a convenient baby-sitter or where it serves as a passive and insidious consumer of time.

We in Ireland could benefit considerably from this timely address.

The Sex Education Debate

From a Christian point of view there are two extremes to be avoided in the realm of sex education. Firstly, there are those who wish to impart, for whatever reason, a sex education devoid of any value other than the purely physical or biological.

Secondly, there are those who see in each and every form of sex education a threat to the faith and morals of the young. It is regrettable that this latter group should attempt to prop up its obscurantist notions by appealing to the teaching of the Catholic Church.

Let us be perfectly clear on what the official teaching of the Catholic Church is on sex education. In 1930 Pope Pius XI emphasised the positive value of sex education when it is given by those "who have received from God the educational mission and grace of state".

This positive value of sex education has been developed gradually by successive pontiffs. Pope Pius XII, for example, pinpointed the responsibility of the family in this area: sex education ideally should be imparted within the ambit of the home.

All of this papal teaching, as well as that of the Second Vatican Council, has been summarised and developed further in a document issued in November 1983 by the Congregation for Catholic Education in Rome.

This document gives the Church's answers to the WHY, WHO, WHEN, WHERE, WHAT and HOW of sex education and is required reading for anyone who wishes to invoke the teaching of the Catholic Church in this sensitive area.

There is no doubt left in anyone's mind as to the ideal: sex education is best given by the parents. This is stated several times. So, too, are the difficulties encountered in reaching this ideal.

Parents often feel quite inadequate and delegate the responsibility to other people or agencies—the priest, for example, or the school. In many cases, however, the necessity of such an education is not adverted to by parents.

So far we have three possible approaches to sex education on the part of parents: (1) the parents themselves teach their children (2) the parents ask another person or agency to perform this task for them (3) the parents aren't aware of the need for such an education.

There is a fourth approach where the parents are aware of the need for sex education, are unable to teach their own children, and are unwilling to entrust this task to anyone else.

"Children will learn about sex soon enough. They will pick it up as they go along!"

They certainly will! Young people will learn "the facts of life" from two sources— either from other young people with whom they associate (and then it is usually a case of the blind leading the blind) or they will get their education in sexuality from "the hidden persuaders", the mass media. In this case they will be taught—and will not even know what they are being taught—certain values, or non-values, relative to human sexuality. Pope John Paul II singles out "the small screen" of television for special attention in this regard:

> Fascinated and devoid of defence before the world and adults, children are naturally ready to accept whatever is offered to them, whether good or bad. They are attracted by the "small screen", they follow each gesture which is portrayed and they perceive, before and better than every other person,the emotions and feelings which result.

Let us be under no illusion. Children will get their sex education one way or the other. A great responsibility rests on the parents to impart this type of knowledge themselves, or to entrust the task to others whom they judge competent.

Which reminds me of the story which is told of the father who was very reluctant to tell his young son the facts of life. Urged to do so by the mother of the family, who was expecting the imminent arrival of their second child, the father finally sat down with his young son and with a mixture of dread and reticence launched into the story of how the youngster should prepare himself for the arrival of the stork any day now.

"I hope the big bird doesn't frighten Mammy," replied the boy. "You see, Daddy, she's about eight months pregnant at the moment!"

Wit and Womanhood

"God save us from sullen saints," was the constant prayer of one of the really great women in the history of the Church. The day of my writing this is the feast of St Teresa of Avila, who died over 400 years ago, and who was described by one historian as being "always one step ahead of the Inquisition."

To remember Teresa is to celebrate her *wit* and *womanhood*.

The story is told of how the saint was cooking one day when she was suddenly raised upwards by God's power.

"Lord," she prayed, "if you're going to lift me up, you're going to have to lift the pan, too!"

And on another occasion she tells of complaining to God in prayer about a particularly difficult superior.

"Lord," she prayed, "if I had my way that woman would never be Superior of this community."

"Teresa," she tells us she heard the Lord reply, "if I had my way, she wouldn't be either!"

God knows we could all do with an injection of Teresa's sense of humour today. We, as a nation, are in danger of losing that great quality. I am not talking about being funny. There is nothing particularly funny about a small country where unemployment is heading toward the quarter million mark and where killing and maiming are daily events.

I am talking, rather, about an ability to laugh at ourselves, to see things in perspective, not to take ourselves so seriously all the time.

There is a venom, a viciousness creeping into our national discourse. This is manifested in many ways—in an unwillingness to listen to the other's point of view but, on the contrary to ridicule and caricature his or her opinion and then to demolish one's own caricature.

There is something ugly about our indecent curiosity with regard to the private lives of prominent citizens and a willingness on the part of a small section of the media to cash in by catering to this curiosity.

I'm afraid "the informer" is back with us again: he or she who is only too willing to be the eyes and ears which spy fellow citizens and neighbours and who supplies the information—more often misinformation—to those too ready to use it.

What can one do to help a person whose good name has been shattered by inneundo, by "the wink-and-elbow language of delight?"

Maybe some type of "Ministry for Truth" or some new religious order is needed, which will be as dedicated to caring for those downtrodden and damaged in character—and consequently in spirit—as other ministries and orders are concerned for the broken in mind and body.

Each age likes to think of itself as sophisticated. Today's exasperated feminists have a fondness for describing some chauvinist attitudes to women as "mediaeval." In doing so they are insulting the mediaevalists!

The truth is that St Teresa lived towards the end of an era in history where the position of women was described as: *Nec domina, nec ancilla, sed socia.* ("Not mistress, not servant, but companion"). The famous French scholar and archivist, Regine Pernoud says of that period: "Women were entirely integrated into everyday life."

The fact that Saint Teresa has been given "an honorary Doctorate" in the Church should not blind us to the fact that she was a truly liberated lady who never suffered fools gladly, especially if they were ecclesiastical fools.

One such person, a prelate, paid her a visit and found the saint eating partridge. He expressed his disapproval of a woman famous for her holiness taking such obvious relish in good food.

"What a scandal! What would people say!"

"Let them say what they please," Teresa answered. "There is a time for penance and a time for partridge!"

He would be blind who could not read "the signs of the times" and work for, and welcome the liberation of women, wherever this is happening. The Second Vatican Council listed the acknowledgement and promotion of women's equality, political and social, as "an urgent duty of Christians in regard to culture." (*Church in the Modern World* 60)

The excessive assertiveness of some women in the feminist movement, on the one hand, and the conscious or unconscious blindness of some men, on the other hand, should blind no one to the fact that the struggle for the equality of women is one of the great Christian projects of our time.

It is not good enough to shrug off this struggle as the work of extremist groups.

"Rumour has it that this is the age of the liberated woman, the progressive woman, the superwoman. A look at comtemporary society would make it seem like a media myth and the labels so much advertising jargon."

Words of an extremist? Indeed not, but of Mrs Nano McDonald, speaking as National President of the Irish Countrywomen's Association.

Exhorting women "once and for all to stop resisting our own emancipation" Mrs McDonald listed the rights of women to health and education and their involvement in Government and State bodies as areas in which the struggle for the equality of women can be carried forward.

It would be at our own peril that we would turn a deaf ear to the pleas of such a good and committed Christian woman. It is the task of all of us to identity and work for the removal of that discrimination which has made woman "the peg on which the wit hangs his jest, the preacher his text, the cynic his grouch, and the sinner his justification".

St Teresa, most practical of women, pray for us.

A Journey in Faith

A certain poor woman in a far land was greatly saddened by her inability to conceive a child. A neighbour told her of a holy man with power to work miracles who was visiting a neighbouring land, and so she set out in search of this great wonderworker.

When she arrived at the city where he was reputed to be, he had moved on to another town, and so she followed him from town to town, from city to city, and from land to land until she at last caught up with him.

He received her graciously and listened attentively to the woman's story. When she was finished, he asked her: "What sacrifice do you intend to make in return for such a great favour from the Lord?"

"I am a poor woman with no worldly possessions," she replied, "but I do have one treasure at home which has been passed down from one generation to another. It is a bridal dress of great beauty and worth."

"Bring it to me," the holy man ordered her.

And so the poor woman set out for home again and once more, this time with the only thing in all the world she possessed, followed the holy man's path over many days and weeks and months.

When she finally caught up with him, he simply accepted her offering, blessed her and sent her home. Within a year of her reaching home, she gave birth to a baby boy.

In the same village there lived another woman who also desired greatly to give birth to a child. But after many years of marriage, she, too, had come to realise that such a blessing was not to be her lot.

Greatly encouraged by the good fortune and story of her fellow townswoman, she, too, packed her precious bridal dress and set out in search of the holy man. She, too, journeyed many months from place to place, arriving in a city to discover that the had gone on to the next town.

She finally caught up with him, told her story. The old man listened to her with great kindness, and she offered her only earthly treasure.

With great sadness the old man confessed that he would be

unable to help her. Greatly perplexed, she replied: "But you helped my townswoman and I did everything she did. Why can't you help me? What's the difference between her and me?"

"The difference," replied the holy man, "is that she had no story to go by when she set forth on her journey!"

Two Roads

A student I once taught joined Mother Teresa in India and is now in charge of a large leper colony there. Part of his daily task is to distribute medicine not only to the unfortunate patients under his care but also to go round in his jeep distributing medicine and other supplies to those poor unfortunate lepers who have not been able to get a place in the hospital and who camp out on nearby hills.

Each day they gather at selected points to receive their supplies. One day, the priest told me, there were simply no medicines to distribute so he sent an assistant, a leper himself, to the various assembly points, to inform the people that supplies had run out but that distribution would resume as normal on the following day. When the priest himself went out again with supplies, he noticed that the lepers were not as friendly as usual. When he inquired what the reason was, they told him they were disappointed that they had not received a visit the previous day.

"But didn't you see the notice I sent out?" he inquired.

"We did," he was told, "but you should have come anyhow!" That priest told me he learned more about the priesthood and religious life from that one exchange than he did on all the spiritual seminars and retreats he had ever undertaken.

"You should have come anyhow!" The message was quite simple. "We value you for who you *are* and not just for what you *do* for us or what you *give us*."

In today's world, we are being tempted to be "relevant", but to be "relevant" in the way that the Son of God was relevant, people must come ahead of programmes, and God must come ahead of all. It is not a question of either/or; it is a question of what grounds our life, our ministry and our apostolate. My own plans or God's will?

It is no secret to anyone that many priests and religious today are asking themselves very searching questions, indeed:

- What is the meaning of my life?
- Did I make the right decision?
- Am I doing anything really useful with my life?

They see many who have left the priesthood and the religious life.

They see their own sisters and brothers with families and careers and can only see very little proof of the good they themselves are doing. Hardly a day goes by without some sort of criticism or outright attack on their way of life or their performance. There is a great deal of confrontation in their lives and those Irish people who appreciate their efforts are shy enough and slow enough to come forward with the odd word of praise.

The values and virtues which priests and religious pursue seem old fashioned and out of place in a world which prides itself on freedom. "Chastity," "celibacy," "obedience," "sacrifice" are words which do not appear much in everyday language. The world in which we live no longer finds such virtues and values "relevant", if it ever did.

When religious forget that all they do must be rooted in their consecration and in their vowed life, when priests forget that all their life and work derives its value from their discipleship with Christ, then indeed is addressed to us the condemnation of Christ himself: "Get behind me, Satan, for you are a scandal in the Church!"

To get behind Christ means to take one's proper place, to order correctly the priorities in one's life, not to "lose the run of oneself" and engage in the creation of one's own kingdom or a kingdom of this world. Ours is the task of promoting the kingdom of God; it is kingdom which is *in* this world but never *of* it.

All of us—lay, religious and clergy—have made choices. In making a choice, we exclude from our lives several other choices. It is not only priests and religious who are called to do this. When one marries, one marries one other person and, in doing so, decides not to marry several others. When one decides to live the single life, one decides against marrying anyone.

The American poet, Robert Frost, once wrote about this:

> *Two roads diverged in a yellow wood.*
> *And sorry I could not travel both*
> *And be one traveller, long I stood*
> *And looked down one as far as I could*
> *To where it bent in the undergrowth;*
>
> *I shall be telling this with a sigh*
> *Somewhere ages and ages hence:*
> *Two roads diverged in a wood, and I—*
> *I took the one less travelled by,*
> *And that has made all the difference.*

May the road you have chosen, whether married or single, whether priest or religious, make all the difference in all that you are and all that you do, and may God grant you the strength to walk that road with hope in your hearts, joy in your spirits, and a spring in your step.

What's in a Job?

Have you noticed how many winners of the Lottery declare their intention of continuing on with their work after their great stroke of luck? Common sense seems to prevail and at least there is the declared intention of not allowing a sudden inflow of money to disturb the rhythm of life, especially working life.

You mightn't think that too strange, but I find it greatly encouraging. After all, you would think that the arrival of a cool quarter of a million punts on the doorstep some morning would cause a sudden rush of blood to the head.

In fact, some people do worry about what such a sudden windfall might do. To others, of course, never to themselves. In fact, there is the story of some people who learned that one of their neighbours had won something in the nature of a half million punts.

Kathleen had a rather serious heart condition and her neighbours and friends were extremely concerned about the effect that it might have on her and prevailed upon the local priest to visit her with a view to breaking the news gently to the good lady.

"I wonder," began the priest tentatively, "what would your reaction be, Kathleen, if you were to win the big prize in the lottery."

"Well, Father," Kathleen replied, "I'm not that interested in money and you know as well as I do that I buy the odd ticket now and then just to have a little interest in the thing."

"I know that, indeed, but, if you were to win the big prize what would you actualy do with it?" persisted the priest.

"God has been good to me, Father, as you well know. I have raised the children and, thank God, they're all in good jobs. I have all I want and the best of neighbours, and to tell you the truth, if I were ever to win the big prize I'd hand the whole thing over to yourself, Father."

Whereupon the priest had a heart attack!

But there is a more significant and, indeed, hopeful note to the determination of lottery winners to hang on to their jobs. They are saying something very important about work itself.

Father John C Haughey has written recently about the idea of finding out how workers felt about their work. It is too often taken for granted that work is just a means to achieve largely private ends, but work, he suggests in an article in the Jesuit magazine *America*, can have many different interpretations.

First of all, work can mean just a job I do merely to obtain money so that I can do the things that I feel are really worthwhile in life. The job in itself has no meaning. It brings me the means by which I can raise a family, achieve status, etc.

For others a job is just a job. It happens to be whatever I am at now. It has no particular relevance or meaning and I don't bring any relevance or meaning to it. I just work.

Thirdly, work is drudgery, something I do because I have to do it. If I were to give it any particular meaning beyond itself, I would see it, perhaps, as the result of original sin, as in Genesis, "By the sweat of your brow shall you get bread to eat."

The US Bishops pastoral on the economy interpreted work (a) as a means of self-expression and self-realisation, (b) as a way of making ends meet, and (c) as a way of contributing to the well-being of the community.

Pope John Paul went back to Genesis and came up with a religious significance to work. People are created in the image and likeness of God and share with him in the ongoing creation of the world.

The founder of the Young Christian Workers, Cardinal Joseph Cardijn called the workbench "an altar on which the lay priesthood prolongs the sacrifice of the Mass", a thought reminiscent of St Paul's plea: "I beg you to offer your bodies as a living sacrifice holy and acceptable to God, your spiritual worship."

There are other ways of looking at one's work. As a service, for example. Jesus came as one who serves. The Christian's work in the world continues that service of Christ to others. Every time I sit down to meals the prayer I say reminds me of the truth that the food and drink set before me is given me by God through the work of human hands.

Finally, and this list of ways of looking at one's work makes no claim to be in any way exhaustive, work for many is viewed as vocational. That is, my vocation in life is to be a nurse, a doctor, a mother, a priest, and all my work is viewed in this particular light.

Pope John Paul in his encyclical letter *On Human Work* presents a vision of the person at work that is immensely inspiring and challenging. Commenting on that vision, one writer, Alfred T Hennelly, had this to say:

Suppose all the enormous energies of so many persons in the Church were understood, not in the utilitarian mode just mentioned that is so common in our society, but as a real continuation to the development of the kingdom of God.

Suppose the act of work, whatever its nature, were seen as a creative act, in union with God the Creator, that acutally builds up the earth and helps to form a new human family.

Suppose, finally, that all this toil and labour were viewed as very concrete ways of continuing the redemptive activity of Jesus Christ, a specific mode of dying and rising with him. The latter idea is one which often remains on an abstract or unintelligible level for the ordinary believer.

If these things did occur, it is clear that the "spiritual life" of millions of people would be expanded to include not only the traditional and necessary activities of prayer, contemplation and worship but also what can be the dull routine or the exhilarating satisfaction of the daily round of work.

One cannot read this without realising the immense tragedy and sufferings of those who seek employment without success.

And the next time one hears a lottery winner expressing the intention of not giving up work to enjoy his or her good fortune, realise that you are listening to one who has a far more Christian interpretation of work than he or she might realise or even admit.

Service and Servility

A few words about Pope John Paul's encyclical, *On Human Work*.

In that letter the Pope introduces into his analysis of unemployment a distinction between the *direct* and the *indirect* employer. The direct employer, that is, the employer in the usual sense of the word, is the person or corporation who makes a contract with the worker in regard to work to be done and payment to be received.

The indirect employer, on the other hand, takes in all those social factors which influence the contract between the worker and the direct employer and includes such things as government legislation affecting conditions of employment, training of workers, systems of transport and communications, housing etc.

The problem of unemployment can only be solved if the reality and importance of the indirect employer is given due recognition and attention. I intend to single out what I consider to be one very important element in this so-called indirect employer in our country. *I refer to our attitude to work and in particular to service.* The reason I do so is because of the importance of the service sector in any attempt to solve our national crisis.

In brief, our attitude to service in this country must change if there is to be any great growth in the number of people employed in that sector.

It is my belief that in this country we too often confuse *civility* and *servility*, *service* and *servitude*. Perhaps a few examples will help illustrate what I mean, and these examples are taken from real life.

One concerns a couple who recently asked for a bottle of white wine with their meal. The waiter, in what I am assured was a Grade A Hotel restaurant, returned and plonked the bottle on the table and returned to his post. When the husband called the young man back and asked him whether it would be possible to have the wine chilled, the young man took the bottle and sauntered off with it in the direction of the kitchen, but not before making the rather sullen remark, "Isn't it chilly enough outside!"

Another example concerns an employer going to a certain college for the purpose of recruiting some staff only to be told by a prominent member of staff that he, the potential employer, had a reputation of demanding a high qualilty performance from his staff and, because of this, there was no great enthusiasm among the students to come to him for interview. The good news was that they, the students,would be willing to talk with him! That is, the potential employees were willing to interview the employer!

A third example: I refer to the service charge added by our hotels and restaurants. This service charge is called a "tip" or, more properly, a "gratuity".

Gratuity, if I am not mistaken, means something freely given, a little bonus, a little extra to show our appreciation. It takes some stretch of language and imagination to see how one can be constantly charged for what should be given free gratis. This little custom speaks volumes about our attitude to service. What I am suggesting is that under the heading of the "indirect employer" comes the national attitude to service—and I go further to suggest that there is a radical need for all of us to take a look at the quality of such service. The two most frequent lies in Ireland today are: "The cheque is in the post!" and "I'll be there first thing in the morning!"

One last point. Not only can service be of a poor quality all too often, but too frequently we *expect* it to be so, or at least we *tolerate* it. This is also a factor in the "indirect employer" equation. "That's the last time I'm going back to that restaurant, that hotel. The service was terrible." But did I do anything about it? Did I tell the owner or the manager. No, what's the use? But I told all my friends! And what, I ask you is the use of that?

I am convinced that a great deal can be accomplished if more and more of us can look upon service not so much as a favour we bestow on others out of the generosity of our hearts but as something they can rightly expect from us by fact that they have paid for it. Service is the other side of the contract.

Christ Throws A Party at Dawn

Some years ago, when an Irish publisher (not the publisher of this little book!) was compiling a book of homilies for certain occasions, I was asked to write a homily on the death of a young person. I couldn't and didn't.

In 1990 I did write such a homily because a very dear friend of mine died suddenly. Gay Moloney was in his prime when he suffered a massive brain haemorrhage and was dead within 24 hours. As his mother told me: "Gay came into the world quietly, if a little prematurely, on an October Friday and left it just as quietly and prematurely on another Friday in October.

On 31 January, 1986, I officiated at the marriage of the lovely young Patricia Hunter and Gay. One thousand days later many of the same people who made up the wedding party returned to the same church for Gay's funeral. In the hope that they will bring comfort to those who mourn, these are the words I shared with Patricia and all present in Foxrock Church that Monday morning.

They took his body down from the Cross, laid it in the tomb. They rolled the stone into place to seal the tomb. Then they went home.

In those stark words is described the death and burial of a young man whom Christians throughout the world believe is the Son of God. For those who loved him, his death was nonsense and all the good news of Resurrection would take days, weeks, months and years to sink in. For some Christians it still hasn't.

I mention this today because I know that many of you, especially those who knew Gay best, might search for meaning and answers to the *why* of his death at such a young age.

Please don't ask me. I have no more knowledge than you do. I share with you two things this morning: the same sense of awful sadness and loss and the same faith that young Gay Moloney is in safe and loving hands at this very moment.

So please don't ask me *why*. I am not a magician or seer or soothsayer but, like most of you here this morning, a follower of Jesus Christ, the Son of God, who had to go through death to experience the Resurrection.

There are those who on days such as this act as if their belief in the Resurrection should instantly mend broken hearts, dry up all tears, make sense of everything immediately. They are wrong. They forget that Jesus himself wept in the face of the death of a friend of his, even though he was soon to raise Lazarus from the dead.

Faith is *not* about explaining away the reality of death, giving glib answers, offering instant solutions. For life itself and, indeed, death is not a problem to be solved but a mystery to be lived out. Faith is about trusting in a loving God precisely when there are no answers. Faith is about looking death in the eye, accepting it as death, but believing that it is not the last word. Faith is about trusting, not about explaining.

In the Catholic Church, unlike other Christian Churches, we are asked at the funeral mass not to deliver a eulogy. It is a place to call all of us to believe, to hope, to trust. Besides, Gay Moloney needs no eulogy from me. The life of this lovely, vibrant young man is known to the great majority of you. Known certainly to those who matter most—Patricia and Amelia; Ursula, Paddy and family; Betty, Hugh and family; and so many other relatives, friends and colleagues. There is no need for me to search for empty words to describe the beauty of this young life so suddenly ended.

There are a few things I want to tell you, however, and especially you, Patricia. Love is not measured by length of days but by depth of affection and commitment, and there was more love in your 1000 days of married life than in many a marriage of 50 years or more.

Patricia, your love for Gay will never end, and that in itself is the beginning and proof of the Resurrection. For your love is, quite literally, stronger than death and reaches out to Gay beyond the grave.

This is no dead man you love, Patricia, but one who, through the goodness and mercy of God, has followed Jesus into and beyond the grave. And I say to you and all who loved Gay so much what the angel told the women on the morning of the Resurrection:

"Why look among the dead for someone who is alive? He is not here; he has risen!" (Luke 24:5)

One thousand days ago, on 31 January, 1986, when I was

privileged to preside at the marriage of Patricia and Gay, many of you were here in this very Church. It was a day of great joy and after the wedding ceremony we were all looking forward to and had a great day's crack. Many of us are back here again today and the only "crack" is the cracks in the broken hearts of many of us.

On that day I said two things to those attending the wedding: One, you were not here as spectators but as partakers. Well, I say the same to you today and your presence and partaking in the sorrow of Gay's family lightens the load immensely.

The second thing I referred to that day was the presence of a third partner in the wedding ceremony. Three people made vows before this altar that January afternoon: Patricia Hunter, Gay Moloney and God. God was always important in the lives of Gay and Patricia. After all, it was at the folk mass they first met.

To Patricia and to all of you who are broken-hearted this morning I say: continue to trust that third partner. Continue to believe that death has not the last word; that Gay is not here, he is risen.

Be consoled with these Resurrection words of an Irish poet, P.H. Ryan:

> *The world will not believe*
> *The blind see*
> *Cripples running*
> *to our feast,*
> *Widows dance,*
> *Yes, dead men sing,*
> *While all the guests*
> *Eat peace*
> *And drink delight.*
>
> *Christ throws a party*
> *At dawn*
> *And splashes water*
> *In the face of unbelief.*

In Memory of
Father Tommy Kelly

He died thousands of miles from home and alone. He died during the night when fire razed the presbytery where he lived beside the small church which was the joy of his life. He died in Yonezawa City, part of the Yamagata Mission Area of Japan and was laid to rest in Japan far from Ballygar where he was born in the mid 1930's. At the funeral Mass they placed his fishing rod on the altar. He loved the fish. Fishermen seem to make good apostles.

One never hears much about the Japanese missions; there is nothing spectacular happening there from the purely human point of view. Converts are few and statistics tell very little of the story of all the Irish missionaries who work and pray and love and quietly make Christ present in the midst of this ancient people.

I spent many years in the seminary with Father Tommy Kelly. He was droll and quiet and good-natured and more or less unflappable. He was easy-going and ambitious in one sense only— to get to the Japanese missions. He got there in 1960 and I saw him only two or three times after that.

I attended a Requiem Mass for him in Boyle, Co. Roscommon in 1983. His mother and the rest of the family were there. His father was too ill to attend. We celebrated the mass of the Resurrection but in a broken-hearted sort of way. God grant you rest, Tommy, and may the soil of the land you loved and served so well rest gently on your grave.

A group of Japanese people, Christian and non-Christian, decided to remember Fr. Tommy with a little booklet which they entitled *Our Reminiscences Of Father Kelly*. One of the contributors is Suematsu Yaita and here are some of the things he wrote about a good priest.

> Kelly-san, pardon me for addressing you as "Kelly-san" (Mr Kelly) instead of addressing you as Father Kelly. When I was talking to you in English, I said "Father Kelly", but in speaking in Japanese I naturally came to use "Kelly-san." (The Japanese "san" implies dearness.) That's because you were not only an honourable priest, but also as a human

being you were the most broad-minded, deeply attached to us and the best neighbour of ours who did many kindnesses to us all.

When you were going home on leave, you never told us the date and time of your departure, even though many asked you. The answer you gave to everybody was that you hadn't finished packing your things. I dared to ask you: "Really you don't like being seen off by lots of people at the station, do you?" "That's right," was your answer. Kelly-san, I have never heard you find fault with the out-of-date habits and customs of this country, but by starting silently on an endless journey without anyone seeing you off, perhaps you might have criticised old-fashioned customs of ours, such as the scenes of our seeing people off on a large scale at the railroad station when they are leaving for their new jobs after graduation or for their new posts, and those of our seeing off or meeting VIP's in a showy manner at the international airports.

Kelly-san, who was severe enough on himself and gentle enough toward others, always showing smiles on his face . . . We looked forward to having you here in Sakata again. We expected that you would stay forever in this city, if possible, to remain a good neighbour, a good teacher, and a good adviser to us citizens. If it was impossible, we hoped at least to see you smile and hear your jokes once or twice a year. Now the wish has turned out to be a dream owing to the disastrous accident. We can do nothing but regret it and mourn your passing away. But Kelly-san, the footmarks you have left on this district, especially on the town of Sakata, are indeed great. You did a lot for the church and the believers in Christianity, and besides you showed limitless favours to us citizens, a lot of English teachers and their students, and the families of both. Thank you very much. How inconvenient it must have been to you to live alone in a country far from your own! Never did you complain of such daily inconveniences as well as of difficulties in human relations! You were really a man of perseverance none of us equalled. We all appreciate your great endeavours and pains you took while you were alive and again say, "Thank you very much, Kelly-san."

Kelly-san, you have started on an endless journey in an instant, leaving us without saying a word. We can't help lamenting the fact that your departure was lonely this time, too, just like your leaving for home on leave! We can never see you again, Kelly-san, who was gentleness itself! Can you imagine how sad and lonely we feel? However, we shall never forget you. We shall never forget your devotion, self-sacrifice, kindness and humour. These virtues will be deeply impressed in our minds forever as a precious inheritance from you. Kelly-san, you are sure to remain alive in our souls for ever and ever.

May you sleep in peace! Amen.

Faith and Monsignor Horan

We know little about the three wise men who brought gifts from the east to the new-born Christ, but at least this lack of knowledge leaves room for conjuring up what type of people they might have been.

One quality they must have had in abundance was courage—courage to set out on what was a fairly dangerous and adventurous mission, and a courage to do so in spite of the ever-present critics.

Imagine the comments "back home" about the three of them. "Did you hear the latest? Thee chaps have saddled up and are gone off in pursuit of a star! Did you ever hear the likes of it, leaving their families, their jobs, and having no idea exactly what they were seeking or where!"

It isn't difficult to picture the scepticism and the sarcasm which must have been poured over their proposals and their plans. There would be no scarcity of "the wink and elbow language of delight" in their hometown. But they persevered and won a place in history—and not any old history, but the history of salvation.

More importantly, to them was revealed the saviour of the world who in a few years would call for this same type of courage and bravery and initiative in his followers. He would speak, for example, of the danger of a person "playing it safe" and burying the talents God had given him or her.

Somehow I could see the late Monsignor James Horan on one of those camels! I was reminded of him when Aer Lingus applied for a licence to fly into Knock. Knock, imagine! The famous "foggy, boggy airport" that became the only European airport that made a profit in the first year of its existence.

I was reminded of him when Aer Lingus applied for a licence to fly into Sligo. And I was reminded of him again when Aer Lingus applied for a licence to fly into Galway. A couple of years ago the brave Monsignor was derided for daring to suggest that Connacht needed an airport. The "experts" were hauled out and given a good innings in the media for the views that an airport in Connacht would be nothing but a white elephant.

And now there is silence when the possibility of three airports serving the West is suggested. If one airport was so nonsensical, what nonsense must the existence of three be! Yet I haven't heard a sound from the original critics of Knock. The three hardest words to say surely must be: "I was wrong."

To paraphrase a song from my diocese, "God grant you glory, brave Monsignor Horan, And open heaven to all your men!" To me you will always be a member of that gallant group of "wise men" who did what had to be done for your people.

From your place in heaven, pray the good Lord that He will rid our land of one of our greatest evils—begrudgery.

"We Lepers"

"The political and journalistic world can boast of very few heroes who compare with him. It is worthwhile to look for the sources of such heroism", wrote Mahatma Gandhi.

It is reported that Mother Teresa of Calcutta has on several occasions petitioned the Holy Father to canonise him. When reminded that the requisite miracles have not been presented, the same nun is reported to have replied that one of the greatest miracles of our times must surely be the fact that lepers are no longer considered outcasts from today's society.

It is believed that he is one of the few, perhaps even the only person whose beatification and canonisation has been sought by every Catholic Bishops' Conference in the world.

A leading American journal captioned one of its recent articles with the headline: *Aids—Another Damien Needed*. For that is the "he" in the paragraphs above: Joseph de Veuster, born at Tormeloo, Belgium on 3 January, 1840, ordained in Honolulu on 21 May, 1864, died 15 April, 1889.

A short life, indeed, just some 49 years, but a life which captured and continues to capture the admiration of the world, Catholic and non-Catholic, Christian and non-Christian alike.

As a child I was fascinated by the life story of this real-life hero as, I'm sure, were many of my age. At 19 years of age Fr Damien, the name in religion chosen by Joseph de Veuster, entered the Congregation of the Sacred Hearts. I entered the same Congregation at the same age and I remember well seeing a film on Damien's life during my first few days in the Novitiate in Cootehill. One scene, in particular, remained with me for the rest of my life.

It showed a tired priest, at the end of a long day, washing his weary feet in a small basin of water. In fact, the basin was so small that he was able to wash only one foot at a time.

He had finished washing one foot and when he put his other foot into the basin, he was forced to take it out immediately; the water was scaldingly hot.

And then the terrible truth dawned: the priest had contracted leprosy. Switch to the next morning at Mass and watch Fr Damien kissing the book of the Gospels, laying it down and commencing his sermon with two simple words: "We lepers..."

Two words which flashed around the world and focused the attention of mankind on what, up until then, no one wanted to know. But let Damien himself describe the reality in which he found himself.

> Shut up in a corner of the island of Molokai, between inaccessible cliffs and the sea, these unfortunate creatures are condemned to perpetual exile. Out of two thousand in all, who have been sent here, some eight hundred are still living, and among them a certain number of Catholics. A priest who should be placed here must consider himself shut up with lepers for the rest of his life. Consequently on 11 May, 1873, a steamer landed me here, together with 50 lepers, whom the authorities had collected in the island of Hawaii.

He was 33 years of age at the time and he had no illusions. He referred to his volunteering to go to Molokai and the lepers as a type of death, but with what life his remaining 15 years were lived!

In a letter to his brother, Pamphile, also a priest in the Congregation of the Saced Hearts—in fact, Damien stepped in for Pamphile at the very last moment when the latter was too ill to go on the missions—he describes a day in his life.

> Picture to youself a collection of huts with 800 lepers. No doctor. Every morning after my Mass, which is always followed by an instruction, I go to visit the sick. On entering each hut, I begin by offering to hear their confession. Those who refuse this spiritual help, are not therefore refused temporal assistance, which is given to all without distinction. As for me, I make myself a leper with the lepers, to give all to Jesus Christ.

Even at night he was with his beloved lepers for the cemetery, church and priest's house formed one enclosure. He spoke of keeping watch at night over "this garden of the dead, where my spiritual children lie at rest."

He was soon to lie among them at an age at which he should have been in the prime of life.

> Leprosy has attacked me. There are signs of it on my left cheek and ear, and my eyebrows are beginning to fall; I shall soon be quite disfigured. As I have no doubt of the real

character of the malady, I remain calm, resigned, and very happy in the midst of my people.

And dying, five years after contracting the disease, on 15 April, 1889. The rest, as they say, is history. His remains were returned to Louvain in May 1936 and placed in the crypt of the church where he first entered religious life.

On 15 April, 1969, Father Damien's statue was unveiled in the Statuary Hall of the State Capital in Washington, DC. He was chosen as one of the State of Hawaii's two representatives there. Pope Paul VI declared him "Venerable" on 7 July, 1977.

Many are surprised that he has not been canonised long, long ago. Most people think he has, and that says something. Personally, I sometimes think that he has it so arranged that he will never be officially canonised until his body is returned to that "garden of the dead, where my spiritual children lie at rest. My greatest pleasure is to go there to say my beads, and meditate on that unending happiness which so many of them are already enjoying".

Remembering John Charles

The media interest in Archbishop Lefebvre inevitably threw up a few newspaper articles which focused on the Archbishop's links with Ireland and, in particular, on his friendship with the late Archbishop John Charles McQuaid. A friend of the late "John Charles" (as he was known, even in those pre-Vatican II days) talked to me about the relationship between him and the French archbishop.

It seems that they had many things in common apart from being brothers in the same religious society of the Holy Ghost Congregation. Both loved and held fast to the old ways and both were not always pleased with the way life in the Church developed in the wake of the Vatican Council.

But here, Archbishop McQuaid's friend insisted, their ways parted. The Irishman may not have been personally attracted to everything that came out of the Second Vatican Council but he was obedient to the very end of his life. It was a quality which he shared with all great Church men and women, an obedience and a loyalty which sprang from a profound faith in the Lord's presence in the Church until the end of time.

One need not *understand* everything that is happening in the Church. One need not *like* it. But, great Church man that he was, John Charles McQuaid possessed a loyalty which transcended likes or dislikes, personal opinions, preferences and the like.

An example of this attitude was his response to a question directed at him shortly after his retirement. It is no secret that he was disappointed with the speed with which his resignation was accepted by the Holy See. Asked whether he was sad, he replied simply to his priest-friend: "Sad, Father? How can one be sad when one is doing the will of God? No, Father, not sad. Maybe a little lonely, but not sad."

Anecdotes about the man abound. For example, about his great love of children, especially poor children, and their friendship with him, not to mention the ready access always afforded them. One such youngster arrived for a visit during a meeting of the Conference of Irish Bishops which the Archbishop was hosting at Drumcondra.

On being told that his friend, the Archbishop, was attending a very important meeting, the youngster insisted that a note be sent informing His Grace of his presence. To the surprise of some members of staff, John Charles left the meeting and spent a considerable amount of time with his young friend.

Asked afterwards by a priest who was close to him why he would leave such an important meeting to spend so much time with a youngster, the Archbishop replied: "Father, young people, once rebuffed, never return. Bishops always come back!"

A certain committee was asked to raise money for the archdiocese and was singularly unsuccessful. Archbishop McQuaid allowed a considerable length of time to pass before he requested a meeting with the members. Asked why they had no success in their fund-raising efforts, the chairman informed John Charles that they could not come up with any fund-raising scheme which would be in keeping with the dignity of the archbishop. After all, any raffle or the like in aid of the archdiocese would be closely linked with His Grace and would not be a sufficiently dignified effort. "Gentlemen," the archbishop informed the committee, "in all my years as a priest and bishop I have never found a dignified way of raising money!"

Money was the least of his worries. "If your idea comes from God," he would tell anyone coming to him with a proposal, "then God will provide the money." And God did! He laid great emphasis on discerning whether or not an inspiration came from the Holy Spirit. He was truly a "Holy Ghost man".

"Father," he told the same priest friend who is the source of these little anecdotes, "always wait and see if the idea is from God". "But, Your Grace," asked the priest on one occasion, "how am I to know whether or not a particular idea or plan comes from God and not from some other source?"

"Wait, Father," replied John Charles. "If the idea is God's, then the devil will make strenuous efforts to prevent action on it; he will stir up great opposition to it. This is one indication that God is the author. But the devil will do more. He will use good men to oppose the plan, good men who mean well and think they are acting for the good of the Church. When good, decent men oppose you, then you can be almost certain that the prompting comes from God!"

He even cited one example from his own experience as archbishop, namely, the decision to set up the Blessed Sacrament Chapel in D'Olier Street, in Dublin. Good men from a very reputable organisation (which in the interest of charity and peace will be nameless, opposed him). They not only opposed him but also are believed to have reported him to Rome for bringing the Church into disrepute by turning an upmarket restaurant into a chapel.

And one last story of a great man which has been recorded for posterity in a book by Fr Joe Dunn of Radharc. The book is entitled *No Tigers in Africa* and the affection and respect of the author for Archbishop McQuaid is evident throughout.

Radharc was in its infancy and had not yet ventured overseas. Such a new departure would require permission from Drumcondra and the brave Fr Dunn wrote requesting same. To bolster his case he explained that RTE had agreed to help finance the trip by agreeing to buy any film of wildlife, tigers, elephants, lions, etc., which the Radharc team might make while they were out in Africa committing the Irish missionary story to film.

Fr Dunn has a photocopy of Archbishop McQuaid's reply. It was short and to the point—as always. Permission was granted, but an extra sentence was added, a rare enough occurrence in a letter from the Archbishop. "No tigers in Africa," it simply read. And, of course, there weren't . . .

Archbishop John Charles McQuaid would have been saddened by many events in the life of Marcel Lefebvre and the Church he loved so well. Alike they may have been in many ways, but from the fund of stories I have heard of the late archbishop of Dublin I suspect that John Charles was blessed with that sense of humour which helped him avoid the danger of taking himself too seriously.

He had a wry humour which allowed him to see the irony of life, which allowed him to be gently amused at himself. There is nothing hilariously funny about having a sense of humour. Or a sense of faith, for that matter.

Remembering JFK

In the diocese of Ferns there is a priest, much beloved by all, who will be remembered for his sense of shrewd judgement during the historic visit of President Kennedy to Ireland. The scene was Wexford town and the desire of all and sundry was to get a word and a handshake with the great man himself. The question was: "Where would be the most strategic place to locate oneself?"

No one noticed our friend slip away from his companions and take up his place with a group of nuns who were among the thousands who lined the streets to give the young US President a mighty "Welcome Home" to the county his great-grandfather left so many years before.

Sure enough, as soon as JFK saw the nuns, over he came for a very special word with them. I was teaching in a secondary school in Los Angeles at the time, and the incident came as no surprise to me. Our priest friend knew his man, and must have read that JFK rarely if every passed up an opportunity to greet a group of religious women.

"Why the nuns?" you might ask. Part of the reason might have been the fact that the President's mentally handicapped sister has been cared for all her life by religious sisters. But the President gave a more political reason on more than one occasion.

"Nuns," he said, "always vote for the Democrats; priests, but especially bishops, vote Republican!" He was right. In the waves of nostalgia which swell up on every Kennedy anniversary, it is sobering to remember that many of those who fill acres of print with their memories of 22 November, 1963, voted for Richard Nixon.

They did so for many reasons: some because they thought he would make a better President; others because they thought that it was "too soon" for a Catholic to run for the White House; still others because they were the kind of bigots to whom John Fitzgerald Kennedy addressed this rebuke:

"I believe in an America where religious intolerance will some-day end—where all men and all churches are treated as equals—where every man has the same right to attend or not attend the church of his choice. This is the kind of America I believe in—and this is the kind I fought for in the South Pacific, and the kind my brother died for in Europe."

Bishops—with a few notable exceptions, especially Cardinal Cushing of Boston—were not among JFK's favourite people. Looking back now on that closely-contested Presidential election campaign it is difficult to imagine the Cardinal Archbishop of New York riding around the city in an open car with Kennedy's opponent, Richard M Nixon, two days before the election.

And all this took place in the great Republic where the first commandment is that Church and State are separate. Could you imagine the "crack" some of our native scribes would have if an Archbishop of Dublin were to ride around a Dublin constituency with Charles J Haughey on the eve of a national election! It would be enough to make the Mother and Child Scheme look like a nursery rhyme.

It is no wonder that JFK, on the reviewing stand at his inauguration, is reported to have muttered with obvious glee to the Boston Cardinal, "I hope that Cardinal Spellman is watching this!"

I met Senator Jack Kennedy in 1959. Joe Dowling from Monasterevin, Seamus Mitchell from Ballygar and I went to the US Capitol and were ushered into a waiting-room already filled with people waiting to see the Massachusetts senator for one reason or another. We three were students at the Catholic University of America at the time.

He came right across the room towards us and started talking about Ireland and its balance of payments. Balance of payments! God help me, but at the time I didn't know that Ireland had any, either payments or balance, that is. He was almost shy and got very embarrassed when he couldn't think of the word, "ordination". He was much taller than I had anticipated, his hair was much redder, and he was very low-key, gracious and kind.

He wanted to know whether he could do anything for us and we aksed him could we meet Bobby. He called the Senate Commission which was investigating the Teamsters Union at the time, but it was not in session, and there was no sign of Robert.

He gave us passes for the Senate, tickets for the Senate under-ground railway and said good-bye. We went into the Senate and watched Lyndon Baines Johnson put on one of his masterly performances.

In the years after that I watched John Kennedy's career with special interest. I was supervising a class break at Damien High

School, La Verne, California, when news of his death reached us. With a numbed nation I sat and watched one nightmare scene follow another over the following long days and nights.

Many times since that November day in 1963 John Fitzgerald Kennedy has been assassinated again and again. This time his character has been murdered and there is no question that there is more than one involved in this conspiracy.

I never cease to be amazed at the revelation that it seems to be those people who blame the papers for printing rubbish who themselves are only too ready to believe everything they read!

From his grave in Arlington, Virginia, let these words of John Fitzgerald Kennedy himself answer all those who would tear and destroy and defame the dream and the hope and the vision which in a few short years quickened the spirit of a nation and of a world:

"When President Roosevelt was running for a second term, some garment workers unfolded a sign that said, "We love you for the enemies you have made". Well, I have been making some good enemies lately."

In the words of another whose life was so closely linked with the late President and who was also taken from us in his prime, the Reverend Martin Luther King: "They may kill the dreamer, but they can never kill the dream!"

Remembering
Bishop Fergus

The late Bishop James Fergus of Achonry is much missed by his many friends and asocciates. He was retired when I first met him, but one couldn't but notice the affection in which he was held by so many. He had been a bishop for no less than 42 years and retired on St Patrick's Day 1976. His retirement was a happy one. A genial host himself, he was welcomed everywhere.

Bishop Fergus, a native of Louisburgh, Co. Mayo, was consecrated bishop on 4 May, 1947, but Bishop Dignan of Clonfert. The new Bishop's remarks on that occasion are interesting in the light of present-day problems.

In St Mary's Hall, Ballaghadereen, after a presentation of addresses from priests, teachers and public representatives, Dr Fergus spoke of his great pride in belonging to the plain people of Ireland. If Ireland was to prosper, the people must be prepared to stay at home and work hard, and not be lured to great cities, or by the deceptive standards of life in foreign countries.

If Dr Fergus belonged to the plain people of Ireland, then the plain people of Ireland can be very proud of him indeed! There is one endearing story told of him concerning a visit to him by the Secretary of the Department of Education.

Apparently, the latter had some business to conduct with the Hierachy and Dr Fergus was the main contact. The Secretary phoned the Bishop the previous evening to tell him that he just happened to be in the area on a bit of a fishing holiday and would it be all right to drop up to the Bishop's House for a few minutes the following morning. Of course it would, Bishop James assured him.

The following morning, when the Bishop opened the door, there to greet him were the Secretary of the Department and an Assistant Secretary. The latter also "just happened to be in the area on a bit of a fishing holiday". It was obvious that they had come prepared to do business.

Bishop Fergus gave both of them a hearty welcome and ushered them into his sitting room where, to their amazement, sat most, if not all of their Lordships of Connacht. With a twinkle in his eye the Bishop explained to the men from the department that the other

Bishops "just happened" to be in the area also and had dropped in for a cup of tea!

May Bishop James enjoy the peace and the presence of the Risen Christ whom he served so long, so faithfully and with such joy— among the plain people of Ireland.

Thank God for Jägerstätter

On 1 March, 1943 a young farmer wrote a letter to his wife from an army induction centre in Enns, Austria: "Today I am going to take the difficult step." The "difficult step" was his formal refusal to serve in the Nazi army, a decision which would cost him his life. His letter went on to thank hus wife for her love and for the sacrifices she would have to make on his account. He urged her to turn to the Christ of the Garden of Olives in her moments of trial and concluded with the prayer: *Not my will but Thine be done.*

This Austrian farmer, Franz Jägerstätter, was executed on 9 August, 1943. The story of his lonely but determined resistance to the very meaning of Nazi National Socialism deserves retelling at a time when men and women of good will are attempting to discover the demands of conscience in a world living under the constant threat of nuclear holocaust.

Born on 29 May, 1907 in the remote farming village of St Radegund in Upper Austria, Franz Jägerstätter may well become a saint for our times, his life and death witnessing to the conflict that can arise when one attempts to work out one's duty to Caesar and one's duty to God. Franz was faced with these conflicting demands. His local parish priest, for example, visiting him in prison, appealed to him to remember his own welfare and that of his family even while following his personal ideals and principles. The arguments against his stand have a familiar ring to them: military service did not imply an endorsement of the Nazis and their objectives; millions of other good Catholics were already in the service; what special expertise did an uneducated farmer possess to make such a singular judgement? These and other arguments were used on Franz by several German Austrian priests and by at least one bishop in an attempt to "this fine, upstanding and brave young man" to change his mind. More devastating, however, must have been the appeal of his children, sent in the form of a photograph of his three daughters taken on the Feast of Corpus Christi and showing them in their processional dresses holding up a large banner which read: DEAR FATHER, COME HOME SOON.

On 9 August 1943, at midday, Franz, now in Brandenburg prison, was informed that he was to be executed at 4:00 pm that day. He sat down to write a final leter:

Greetings in God, my dearest, beloved wife and all my children . . . I wish to write you a few words of farewell. I beg you again to forgive me if I have hurt or offended you, just as I have forgiven everything. I beg, too, that all others I have ever offended may forgive me . . . May God accept my life in reparation not only for my sins but for the sins of others as well . . . And now, all my dear ones, fare thee well, and do not forget me in your prayers . . . Through God's grace we will soon meet you in heaven.

The Catholic prison chaplain, himself a German, was with Franz to the end and later, on the same day, spoke of him to some Austrian nuns. "I can only congratulate you on this countryman of yours who lived as a saint and has now died a hero. I say with certainty that this simple man is the only saint that I have met in my lifetime."

Lives such as that of Franz Jägerstätter keep alive the real message of Christianity. A simple bronze plaque next to his grave bears this moving testimony to a remarkable man: *Thank God for Jägerstätter. He knew that we are all brothers and that the commands of Christ are essential for everyone. He has not died in vain. May this great love heal our world so that the peace of God may enter the hearts of all. Amen.*

Titus Brandsma

Father Titus Brandsma was born at Oegeklooster near Bolsward on 23 February, 1881. He was the fifth child and first son of Catholic parents, who lived quietly on a farm in the province of Friesland, in the north of Holland.

Little Anno Sjoerd, as he was called, was physically rather frail and of delicate health, but was a very intelligent boy, always restlessly seeking to improve his mind. While still a child, he showed great friendliness to all and an eagerness to help others. These qualities in later years became so marked that, together with his truly amazing apostolic zeal, they may be considered the outstanding characteristics of his remarkable life.

At the age of eleven he expressed the wish to study for the priesthood and his parents, who were to see all their six children, except one, enter religious life, made no objections. On 17 September 1898, he entered the novitiate of the Carmelite order in the monastery of Boxmeer and was given the name of Titus.

Although the Carmelites at that time were little known in the Netherlands, Titus preferred Carmel to other religious Orders because of its tradition of contemplative life and particular devotion to Mary.

Titus Brandsma became Doctor of Divinity at the Gregorian University in Rome. On his return to Holland he was given the task of teaching philosophy to the Dutch Carmelite students. In 1923 he was appointed Professor of Philosophy and Mysticism at the new Catholic University of Nijmegen. In 1932 he was made Rector of the same University. Although he did excellent work in this large field of learning, he was by no means a great scholar only. One may say he was a very learned apostle, with all the emphasis on apostolate.

In spite of very delicate health, he would never refuse anybody who asked for help. His charity was like a fire, which devoured him. When his country was overrun by the Nazis and the freedom of the Church was being threatened, Titus did not hesitate to defend openly the rights of the Church. And when he was sent down to the living hell of Dachau concentration camp, even there his apostolic heart kept on burning.

Three barracks in Dachau were reserved for about 1600 clergy-men. "You will be in hell," a Dachau vereran told Titus when he was assigned to one of the barracks. "There," the prisoner added, "men die like rats." Of 2,000 Polish priests imprisoned there, 850 died before the war's end.

The prisoners' day began at 4.00 am, from which time on guards chased them, exacted extra hours of labour, cut their miserable rations, hounded, beat and bludgeoned them. Work began at 5.30 am and continued until 7.00 pm, with a "lunch" break.

Titus, already suffering from untreated uremic poisoning, con-tracted a severe foot infection. The open sandals which prisoners wore caused his feet to blister and eventually suppurate. At the end of the work day, fellow prisoners often carried him to the barracks. Father Urbanski, a Polish prisoner, who more than once carried him, remembered: "So even-tempered and approachable was he, so cheerful in the midst of disaster, which was threatening us from all sides, that he deeply touched our hearts." Another prisoner recalled: "He radiated with cheerful courage."

Titus continuously exhorted his fellow prisoners: "Do not yield to hatred. Be patient. We are here in a dark tunnel but we have to go on. At the end, the eternal light is shining for us."

In his very last letter home, Titus, broken in body, full of infection, bruised, and with hardly a sound spot within or without, wrote: "With me, everything is fine. You have to get used to new situations. With God's help, this is working out all right. Don't worry too much about me. In Christ. Your Anno."

Titus, although he knew his days were numbered, refused to enter Dachau's hospital. He knew that in that hellish place inhumanity plumbed new depths. Doctors used prisoners for medical experimentations. Many human guinea pigs suffered frightfully before dying indescribable deaths. The few survivors were ruined for life.

Finally, Titus had no choice. He entered the hospital in the early part of the third week of July. He too became a subject for medical experimentation. In the afternoon of Sunday, 26 July, 1942, the doctors in charge of his case ordered him injected with a deadly drug. Within ten minutes, Father Titus Brandsma, who brought happiness wherever he went on this earth—even to Dachau—was dead.

Peter: The First Pope

I was thinking of a certain priest one morning when I was reading yet another "CHOOSING THE NEW ARCHBISHOP" article in one of the newspapers. And I remembered how his parishioners told how he managed to bring a little humour into that sad, sad Sunday following the death of Pope John Paul I, "the smiling Pope".

Fr Joe was as sad as the rest of them and spoke with great affection of the joy, the hope and the laughter the new Pope had brought in 30 short days.

"But," he warned, "good humour, laughter, intelligence, hope, love, and joy are not enough. The next man must have all of these qualities, but in addition our next Pope must be a big, physically strong man!"

And after a short pause for effect, this big, physically strong priest told his people: "So if I'm missing next Sunday, you'll know where I've gone!" The people smiled through their tears.

Somehow, thinking of that good, big, physically strong priest with the great good humour reminded me of the first big, physically strong Pope. A man called Peter. So let's look at the man whom Jesus chose as the first Pope. After all, compared with that task, choosing a bishop or an archbishop would be in the halfpenny place.

Peter's faith was rock-like. In love, he wasn't far behind, but it took him an awful long time to learn how to follow Jesus. In fact, if we read carefully the exchanges between Peter and the Master, there would appear to be some truth to the rumour that Peter's greatest failing was his attempt to convert Jesus Christ.

Take, for example, the exchange (Matthew 16) where Peter spoke out so forthrightly and confessed: "You are Christ the Son of the living God."

"Good for you, Simon, son of John!" answered Jesus. "For this truth did not come to you from any human being, but it was given to you directly by my Father in heaven."

But what happened a moment later when Jesus spoke of his Passion and death? Peter was having none of it. In fact, he prayed that the Father's will would not be accomplished in the life of

Jesus: "Heaven forbid, Lord, that this should happen to you!" You see, Peter had his own plans for Jesus.

The rebuke from Jesus was quick in coming and sharp in tone: "Get behind me, Satan, for you are a scandal."

Why was poor Peter a scandal? Because he thought in ways that were not God's ways.

"Getting behind" Jesus has a far deeper meaning than appears at first glance. To get behind Jesus was to resume being His disciple. As they say in Dublin, Peter "had lost the run of himself", had gone out in front of Jesus. He had to be reminded that his place was in the footsteps of Jesus.

It was a hard lesson for Peter to learn and he was still learning it to the very end of the earthly life of Jesus and, I'm sure, for many years afterwards.

In the garden he drew the sword to restore the kingdom by means which were not of God's kingdom. Again he was reminded that the only thing that mattered was the Father's plans: "Am I not to drink the cup that the Father has given me?"

On yet another occasion he was trying to plan John's life for him. Peter turned to Jesus and said, nodding to John: "Yes, Lord, but what about him?"

This time he was simply told to mind his own business: "If it is my wish for him to stay until I come,' said Jesus to St Peter of St John, "what business is that of yours? Your business is to follow me."

Again, Peter had lost the run of himself and was told to get behind Jesus and resume discipleship—that the follower is never greater than the Master.

It took a long time for Peter to learn, but, oh, how well he learned in the end! His life ended following in the footsteps of Jesus, right up to and on to his own cross. All the blunders, all the mistakes, all the foolishness, all the thinking the way humans think rather than the way God thinks—all of this was forgotten when that great big-hearted man climbed the cross and joined the Master whom he loved with such great depth and passion.

What a saint, what a rock on which to build the Church!

Retaliate First

A certain man needed to mow his lawn but discovered that his mower was broken. He had a neighbour with whom he was on the best of terms, so he decided to ask him for the loan of his lawn mower.

But the more he thought of it, the more reluctant he became to ask his neighbour. "Maybe," he thought to himself, "he's mowing his own lawn. Or, maybe, he doesn't like anyone else using his mower. Or, maybe, if he gives it to me, he'll think he'll have to give it to every Tom, Dick, and Harry in the neighbourhood."

The grass on his lawn was so overgrown, however, that he found himself walking up his neighbour's pathway and ringing the doorbell. As footsteps approached the door, all his doubts and indecision increased once again.

His neighbour, however, was hardly prepared for the greeting he received at his own front door: "You can keep your ould lawn mower! Who asked you for it anyway? The way you go on about it, you'd think the ould piece of scrap was made of gold!"

God Will Provide If . . .

I have been known to complain about the decrease in the number of vocations to the priesthood and the religious life.

So have many others, both lay and religious, all well-meaning.

Vocations are scarce, we say, resources are scarce . . .

"Scarce" is a relative term. I wonder what the reaction of a bishop from many a South American country would be if he were asked to comment on the number of religious in Ireland. I imagine that "bonanza" would be a more likely description of the Irish situation than "scarcity". I'm thinking of one South American bishop in particular who was handed a new diocese recently by the Holy See. The only realistic way of getting around his huge new diocese was by air. Yet, there was no seminary, few churches, no diocesan services, and a mere handful of priests and religious women. The wonder of it is that we have had such numbers in the past, not that we have so few at present.

Past bounty, however, should not lull us into a false complacency. Priests, as well as religious women and men, are getting fewer and older. That's official. So what does the future hold? As in everything else in life we have an option: *watch* things happen or *cause* things to happen. Could I suggest the following agenda.

Firstly, *speak the encouraging word to and about* those already serving the Christian community as priests, religious sisters and brothers. There is a great deal of cynicism in the air, caustic comment, a fiercely critical attitude. A vocation to the religious life or the priesthood is hardly likely to come out of a home where there is scarcely ever a good word to be said about vocations.

I like Mike Murphy's story about a certain family returning from Mass on Sunday and being hugely critical of the performance of the liturgy. Father thought the homily abominable, Mother thought the choir was ghastly, Elder Brother found the whole thing boring, Sister felt that the readers should be properly trained. Ten-year-old Sean alone had a redeeming word to say: "I thought it was very good value for 10p!"

Secondly, the "welfare state" mentality must not be allowed to lull people into the belief that, come what may, *there will always be a priest*, wherever he comes from. Churches without a Sunday Eucharist in parishes, throughout the First and Second Worlds, where only a few years ago two or three priests ministered, stand as all too silent witnesses to such complacency. I find it a very sobering experience to ask people or delegations, who come to complain about curtailment of services due to scarcity of priests, "How many vocations to the priesthood or religious life have come from your parish in the past ten or twenty years?

Thirdly, young people must be challenged personally to consider seriously a calling to serve Christ as a priest or religious. Pope John Paul has this advice to give:

> Do not be afraid to call. Go out among your young people. Go and meet them personally and call them. The hearts of many young people and not-so-young people are ready to listen to you. We must call. The Lord will do the rest. Let us carry out this ministry wholeheartedly.

Fourthly, there is need for greater clarity about *the very nature of priestly ministry and religious life*. It is now more than 20 years since the Vatican Council issued the first of its conciliar documents, the *Constitution on the Sacred Liturgy*. In those 20 years a great deal has happened to bring about the "full, conscious and active participation in liturgical celebrations" by all the faithful for which that document appealed.

In fact, such was the emphasis on the dignity and corresponding responsibility—the term "ministry" is frequently used—of all Christians, a ministry rooted in the vocation shared by all through Baptism and Confirmation, that *the role of the priest and the value of the religious life was questioned*. The desire to recognise the equality of all God's people led some to minimise the unique responsibility of the priest.

The teaching of Vatican II on the difference *essentially* and not only in degree between the ministerial priesthood and the common priesthood of the faithful was often overlooked or forgotten. This confusion of roles has had its effects on the way in which young people decide upon their vocation in life.

Finally, and this is a responsiblility on all of us, people and priest, married and single, young and old, we must simply continue to *do in faith what Jesus asked us to do: pray to the Lord of the harvest that he will send more and more labourers into the vineyard.*

Bethlehem in Brazil

In December 1985 I was privileged to be able to visit the Ferns Mission to Brazil which was opened by the late Bishop Herlihy. The visit convinced me of my decision, made when I was 16, to be a missionary.

Strangely enough, what impressed me most about the Church in Brazil is how similar things are to the Church at home—people worrying and praying to God to become better people, people suffering and dying, people companioning and celebrating, people loving their children with a passion, trying to give them a good start in life. It's all there—the agony and the ecstasy.

I wish that those who have laboured long in South America might find the time to share their experiences with the home Church. It is my equally fervent wish that those who are there for shorter periods or visits, such as myself, should present their experiences as first impressions, as it were.

One thing which is most impressive in Brazil is the role and participation of the laity in the life of the Church. Their participation is outstanding, in the manner in which they prepared for and participated in the Eucharist. Their singing was simply splendid. There was an atmosphere of joy and of being-at-peace in the Lord's house, a spirit of prayerfulness, a very real sense of community, of true Christian charity. One could not help thinking, or hoping: "Why can't we have this at home?"

On the other hand, when I was speaking to the local bishop later the same day, he informed me that the percentage of those attending Sunday Eucharist can be as low as one in every twenty. It is so easy to compare the best of what is happening somewhere else to the worst of what is happening in Ireland.

My stay in Brazil was short, but I took home with me many vivid memories of the Brazilian people, religious and priests. No one can visit Brazil and not be affected, changed, perhaps converted in some real way.

I will always remember my visit to a family living in a shack in the midst of a *favella* or shantytown. The shack consisted of some rough pieces of wood covered with a tin roof, set down along with dozens of other similar structures in the middle of a sharply sloping field.

In this abode lived a bright, cheerful, little woman. The father of her two children had long since abandoned them after making their lives a misery for many years. Outside the thunder roared and the lightning flashed while this brave woman kept running around her "house" positioning all sorts of containers to catch the rain which kept coming through the roof.

In spite of all this, the shack was incredibly clean, as is just about everything and everybody in Brazil. A shack it may be, perched precariously on what the pouring rain was turning into a mud bank. Inside, a beautiful cabinet stood in the middle of the room, flanked by a huge refrigerator, and the ubiquitous television.

Who should be performing on that same TV but Tom Jones! There he was in all his glory singing *The Green Green Grass of Home*! I asked the mother of the family about her home.

She told me that she was born in the north of Brazil, more than a thousand miles from her present home. Before coming south to Sao Paulo she had never seen anything similar to a shantytown in her entire life and she nearly died when she was brought by her husband to live there at first. But home was at least a thousand miles away to the north and for the poor the moon is closer.

It wasn't just the terrible living conditions, she explained, but the violence and the added problems of drugs. Her great dream was to move out into a rented two-roomed apartment. She doesn't think her chances are good . . .

Meanwhile, in downtown Sao Paulo, nearly every second skyscraper houses a national or international bank. Not even New York or London's banks look anything like these. One gets an idea of the wealth of this incredibly rich and beautiful country—and the poverty. A new bank, Mitsubishi, was rising among all the rest, its main storey faced with beautiful marble.

A few miles away a young woman and her two children peer out at the falling rain and wish for a room or two. It's not too far from Bethlehem . . .

Words On My Headstone

I remember being struck by two things as I looked at the writings on the headstone around St Patrick's Cathedral, Armagh, and in the Catholic cemetery there. The first was how young some of the Irish bishops were at the time of their appointment! The second was how "the Northern troubles" were reflected on the headstones by inscriptions such as "MURDERED BY THE B-SPECIALS" on such and such a date.

Did you ever wonder what you would like to see on the headstone over your grave? I never did until recently, and I was prompted to do so not by any great reflection on death and the life hereafter, but rather by a very strange tribute a letter-writer paid me.

I say "strange" because it wasn't meant to be a tribute. On the contrary, it was meant to be a mild complaint, but no-one could have said anything about me that could have brought me greater pleasure. The writer in question scolded: "You put too much emphasis on hope!" And that gave me an idea for an inscription. What could be nicer than: "THEY SAID HE PUT TOO MUCH EMPHASIS ON HOPE"?

Frankly, I never knew that you could place too much emphasis on hope. I was always taught, whether by the teachers who used the Maynooth Catechism or the documents of the Second Vatican Council, that hope, along with faith and charity, were theological virtues. That is, these were virtues that had God for their object.

How could one have too much faith, hope, or charity? For that matter how could one succeed in putting too much emphasis on any virtue? Weren't we taught, long before the Second Vatican Council was ever heard of, *in medio stat virtus*—that virtue of its very nature stands in the middle ground between extremes? Or, to put it another way, virtue, by its nature, avoids extremes—it is impossible to be extreme in being truly virtuous.

Having too much hope is like having too much of God. I can understand my correspondent's fear that too much hope will make us so heavenly indeed that we become no earthly good. But it doesn't work out like that in practice. Spiritual writers advise us to pray or to hope as if it all depended on God, and work as if all depended on you.

Give me a person with real hope, and I'll bet you that he or she

95

will be a person of action. I say *hope*, not *optimism*, for hope is grounded in God: optimism is based on our own and/or others' performance.

The Psalmist proclaims that all this hope is in the Lord. Even the supposedly secularist United States prints *In God We Trust*, and where do they print it? On their currency . . .